CW00746846

BMW M3

The Complete Story

OTHER TITLES IN THE CROWOOD AUTOCLASSICS SERIES

AC COBRA Brian Laban

ALFA ROMEO 916 GTV AND SPIDER Robert Foskett

ALFA ROMEO SPIDER John Tipler

ASTON MARTIN DB4, DB5 & DB6 Jonathan Wood

ASTON MARTIN DB7 Andrew Noakes

ASTON MARTIN V8 William Presland

AUDI QUATTRO Laurence Meredith

AUSTIN HEALEY Graham Robson

BMW 3 SERIES James Taylor

BMW 5 SERIES James Taylor

CITROËN DS SERIES John Pressnell

FORD CAPRI Graham Robson

FORD ESCORT RS Graham Robson

FROGEYE SPRITE John Baggott

JAGUAR E-TYPE Jonathan Wood

JAGUAR XJ-S Graham Robson

JAGUAR XK8 Graham Robson

JENSEN INTERCEPTOR John Tipler

JOWETT JAVELIN AND JUPITER Geoff McAuley & Edmund Nankivell

LAMBORGHINI COUNTACH Peter Dron

LAND ROVER DEFENDER, 90 AND 110 RANGE James Taylor

LOTUS & CATERHAM SEVEN John Tipler

LOTUS ELAN Matthew Vale

LOTUS ELISE John Tipler

MGA David G. Styles

MGB Brian Laban

MGF AND TF David Knowles

MAZDA MX-5 Antony Ingram

MERCEDES-BENZ CARS OF THE 1990s James Taylor

MERCEDES-BENZ 'FINTAIL' MODELS Brian Long

MERCEDES SL SERIES Andrew Noakes

MERCEDES W113 Myles Kornblatt

MORGAN 4/4 Michael Palmer

MORGAN THREE-WHEELER Peter Miller

PORSCHE CARRERA – THE AIR-COOLED ERA Johnny Tipler

ROVER P5 & P5B James Taylor

SAAB 99 & 900 Lance Cole

SUBARU IMPREZA WRX AND WRX STI James Taylor

SUNBEAM ALPINE AND TIGER Graham Robson

TRIUMPH SPITFIRE & GT6 Richard Dredge

TRIUMPH TR7 David Knowles

VOLKSWAGEN GOLF GTI James Richardson

VOLVO P1800 David G. Styles

BMW M3

The Complete Story

James Taylor

THE CROWOOD PRESS

First published in 2014 by
The Crowood Press Ltd
Ramsbury, Marlborough
Wiltshire SN8 2HR

www.crowood.com

© James Taylor 2014

All rights reserved. No part of this publication may be reproduced or transmitted in any form or by any means, electronic or mechanical, including photocopy, recording, or any information storage and retrieval system, without permission in writing from the publishers.

British Library Cataloguing-in-Publication Data
A catalogue record for this book is available from the British Library.

ISBN 978 1 84797 772 4

Typeset by Jean Cussons Typesetting, Diss, Norfolk

Printed and bound in India by Replika Press Pvt Ltd

CONTENTS

INTRODUCTION AND ACKNOWLEDGEMENTS

The massive success and iconic status of BMW's M3 models have been achieved through a brilliant combination of fine engineering and equally fine marketing. The original M3 of 1986 was essentially a homologation special that allowed BMW to go racing in Europe with a high-performance derivative of their compact 3 Series saloon. However, it wasn't long before customers latched onto the car as something far more than that, and BMW responded equally quickly by developing it as a prestige product. Over the years, the M3 wormed its way into the public consciousness as a unique combination of status, design and driving dynamics.

Others have tried to imitate its success, but the M3 has always been able to ride on the worldwide recognition of a strong brand – the M brand, which started as the Motorsport brand from BMW. Very noticeable is that the M logo and signature tricolour have remained unchanged through more than a quarter of a century of M3 production, even though the cars have developed from 4 cylinders, through sweet 6s and on to V8s.

The essence of the M3 has always been a two-door coupé, although this has been supplemented by smaller-selling convertible and saloon versions. Yet for 2014, changes elsewhere in the BMW model range mean that the high-performance coupé will no longer be badged as an M3 but rather as an M4; the M3 badge will be reserved for saloon versions only. So this book takes the M3 story from its origins to a critical turning point, where the M3 brand will in a sense be diluted.

How well it copes with the change is yet to be seen, but there is every reason to think that BMW's high-performance cars will continue their success story.

In putting this story together, I was struck by how much information is still disputed about the M3 ranges of all ages. Perhaps that is part of the enduring appeal of the range – a mystery always helps to add interest. However, I have done my best to unravel those mysteries, drawing on a vast number of often contradictory sources. I don't doubt that there will still be room for improvement and refinement if this book goes to a second edition.

Special thanks go to my old friend, photographer Nick Dimbleby, who managed to unearth some characteristically superb pictures to help illustrate this book. I am also particularly grateful to BMW specialists Munich Legends, who made several outstanding cars available for photography at short notice, and to enthusiast Finnbar Cunningham for making his E36 M3 Saloon available for photographs. Many other pictures have reached me through BMW GB and BMW in Germany and the USA, who also helped with information in some areas. Beyond that, I'll just say thanks to the huge number of BMW M3 enthusiasts who care enough to make a book like this worthwhile.

James Taylor
Oxfordshire, November 2013

CHAPTER ONE

ORIGINS AND CONTEXT

BMW was just ten years into its revival when the Motorsport division was established in 1972. Torn asunder by the Second World War, which had left one of its major factories in the Soviet-controlled eastern sector of Germany, the company made a hesitant comeback in the late 1940s and early 1950s. With an incoherent model range split among bombastic 'Baroque Angel' saloons, slow-selling ultra-expensive sports and GT cars, and economy models that from 1955 included bubble cars, the company lacked a clear identity. It was also seriously lacking in profits.

By the end of 1959 the problem had become a grave one. That December, the BMW Board discussed a proposal to sell the entire company to Daimler-Benz, who needed extra factory space and at that stage were not in the least concerned about BMW as a potential rival. However, the trade unions, the BMW workforce and many of the company's shareholders were not happy about the idea. Among the major shareholders was the industrialist Herbert Quandt, and he set about buying more BMW shares – against all the

RIGHT: **'The most powerful letter in the world' claimed this advertisement, adding that BMW's Motorsport division was a 'trend-setter in the high-performance league'. The M brand has exerted a special fascination for car enthusiasts in the four decades and more since it was established.**

ABOVE: **In the second half of the 1930s, the BMW 328 was the Bavarian marque's sporting flagship. In the black-and-white picture, Ernst Loof is seen winning the 1936 Eifelrennen.**

**The M3 heritage: from left to right are the first-generation E30 model, the E36
of the 1990s, the turn-of-the-century E46 and the E92 coupé.**

advice from his bankers. Once he had nearly 50 per cent of those shares, he approached the state of Bavaria (where BMW was and still is based) and gained its approval for his purchase of the company.

It was a huge financial risk for Quandt, but it paid off. BMW already had plans for a new medium-sized car that would give the company the volume-seller it so badly needed, and Chief Engineer Alex von Falkenhausen was now able to fund the development of these plans to create a new car. The BMW 1500 appeared in 1961 as a 1962 model, and amply demonstrated what BMW could do when given appropriate financial support. Though the car was a four-door saloon, its distinctive sporting character led to strong sales, and on the profits from those strong sales BMW was able to expand its product range.

The old BMW range of the 1950s gradually disappeared as the 1500 (or 'Neue Klasse' – New Class) range expanded with a 1.8-litre derivative of its 1.5-litre engine and then a

2.0-litre as well. The Neue Klasse platform also provided the basis for a new 2.0-litre grand touring coupé in 1965, sold in 2000C and twin-carburettor 2000CS forms. A new 1.6-litre version of the engine provided power for the first models of a shortened, two-door version of the car called the 1600-2 in 1966, and then that car was further developed with the larger versions of the engine. It was the 2002 (2.0-litre, two-door) model of 1968 that really brought BMW to international attention, proving a particular hit in the USA.

THE SPORTING TRADITION

Though BMW lacked the money to become a major force in international motor sport during the 1940s and 1950s, it could look back with some satisfaction on its achievements in the 1930s during which it had developed a highly respected series of sports cars alongside its larger saloons and their convertible equivalents. The key model was the 328, an open two-seater that first appeared in 1936 and used the 2.0-litre engine from the saloon range.

BMW's 328s took more than 100 class wins in international events in 1937, and in 1938 went on to win their class at Le Mans, in the RAC Tourist Trophy and the Alpine Rally, and in the Mille Miglia. In 1939, a 328 won the RAC Rally, and a 328 repeated its class victory at Le Mans and claimed fifth place overall as well. Then in 1940, which became the last year of international competition as Europe devoted its resources to the war, a special Touring Coupé derivative of the 328 won the Mille Miglia.

It would be 1950 before German drivers were allowed to compete again in international motor sport events, but that did not stop enthusiasts from creating a lively racing scene within the borders of West Germany. Among those enthusiasts was Alex von Falkenhausen, who had been a BMW engineer in the 1930s. For a time, he ran his own small business, constructing racing machines based on pre-war (mostly 328) BMW engines. AFM – Alex von Falkenhausen Motorenbau (engine company) – had ambitions beyond the borders of West Germany, and was quite successful too, but the pre-war BMW engine had a limited life in motor sport as newer designs began to appear. By 1954, AFM was a spent force, and Alex von Falkenhausen returned to BMW to run their racing department.

BMW racing at this stage centred on motorcycles, another element in the BMW product portfolio and one that was important in keeping the company afloat during these difficult years. It was not until the arrival of the new 4-cylinder M10 engine in the Neue Klasse saloons that the company seriously considered taking its cars racing again. As Chris Willows explained in *Classic & Sports Car* magazine for March 1989:

> *The 1800 model enabled BMW to re-enter top-line competition. In 1964 Hubert Hahne drove a twin-carb 1800Ti to a number of victories in the European Touring Car Championship, followed by a manufacturers' title in the 2-litre category the following year with an 1800TISA. [The TISA was a 'homologation special' – and when a car maker builds one of these it is quite obviously serious about going racing.] This was repeated in 1966, 1968 and an overall championship victory the following year thanks to the efforts of Dieter Quester who used both the 2002ti and the turbocharged 2002ti/K.*

The M10 engine that lay at the heart of this new-found success was further developed by BMW's Ludwig Apfelbeck, who developed a 4-valve cylinder head for the 2.0-litre version that enabled outputs as high as 280PS. This was tried in Formula 1 cars in the mid-1960s and showed promise, and by the end of the decade further-developed BMW 4-cylinder engines were winning races in single-seaters designed by Dornier and driven by the BMW team of Hubert Hahne, Jacky Ickx, Dieter Quester and Jo Siffert. However, BMW top management terminated the Formula 2 programme at the end of the 1970 season, and there would be no more single-seater BMW racers for the rest of the decade. The enthusiasm for motor sport had not been dispersed, however. It simply re-emerged in another, and ultimately more profitable, form.

A CHANGE OF FOCUS

The early 1970s saw BMW growing up fast. The success of the 1960s models had bred a new confidence, and the new medium-sized 5 Series range that was introduced in 1972 was an assured and even ambitious replacement for the old four-door Neue Klasse models. Three years later, it was joined by the smaller 3 Series range that replaced the much-admired two-door '02' derivatives of the Neue Klasse. Meanwhile, the big 2.0-litre coupés had been gradually evolving into 3.0-litre, 6-cylinder types and were making waves in their own prestigious corner of the market.

Right in the middle of this, BMW's new Chairman, Eberhard von Kuehnheim, persuaded his Board that the company should take competition seriously again. As part of the plan, a new and dedicated competitions department would be set up, and von Kuehnheim chose his recently recruited Sales Director, Robert A. Lutz, to head it. Lutz in turn hired Jochen Neerpasch as Competitions Director in May 1972. Neerpasch was already a big name in motor sport, as he had been running the successful competitions department for Ford in Germany since 1968.

The new department was set up as a self-managed subsidiary of BMW, with the name of BMW Motorsport GmbH (those four initials are the German equivalent of 'Ltd', or limited company). From 1973, the Motorsport division started to use its own distinctive corporate livery of blue, violet and red stripes, and those colours remain part of its branding today, usually seen alongside a chromed capital M. To help establish this branding, the 1974-model BMW 2002 Turbo carried

Early days: competition-prepared versions of the E9 6-cylinder coupés eventually resulted in the legendary 'Batmobile' cars with their distinctive wing spoilers. This example was offered for sale by auctioneers H and H in the UK during 2012.

BMW lebt mit dem Motorsport

BMW ist mit dem Rennsport groß geworden. Menschen und Automobile sind mit ihm gewachsen und von ihm geprägt.
Dem sportlichen Elan entspricht das sportliche Konzept, das sich am Menschen orientiert, im Rennen erprobt und in der Konstruktion verwirklicht.

In diesem Sinn treibt BMW Motorsport.
Mit einer neuen Gesellschaft: der BMW Motorsport GmbH.
Unter neuem Zeichen und neuem optischen Akzent.
Mit dem Ziel, das bessere Automobil zu bauen.

BMW – Freude am Fahren.

decal side-stripes in these colours, indicating to those in the know that it was a product of the Motorsport division.

In these first few years, the Motorsport division's job was to prepare race engines, race-tuning kits, and special body and chassis parts for both private entrants and for the works team. This latter featured 2002 models and the big coupés, of which the most memorable were undoubtedly the 3.2-litre (and later 3.5-litre) CSL 'Batmobiles' with their Motorsport side-stripes and huge aerodynamic spoilers. The Motorsport division itself was meanwhile struggling for space within BMW's main factory complex in Munich. Not until later would it be granted its own dedicated premises, but in the meantime its remit was gradually extending. It was the Motorsport team who were called upon to construct special-order cars based on mainstream production models. From 1974, for example, customers who knew how to ask the right questions could have their E12 525 or 528 models equipped with the 3.0-litre, 6-cylinder engines otherwise available only in the big 3.0-litre coupés.

LEFT: **A works-prepared BMW saloon, wearing the distinctive three-colour striping of the Motorsport division, dominates this early 1970s advertisement for the then newly formed competition arm of BMW.**

RIGHT: **Successors to the E9 coupés were the E24 6 Series cars. It was not long before one was given the full Motorsport treatment and introduced as a range-topping model. This is the original M 635 CSi, proudly displaying the badge of the Motorsport division on its grille.**

ABOVE: **The first complete car produced by the Motorsport division was the M1 Coupé, seen here at the back of the photograph. It had no 'ordinary' BMW equivalent. In front of it are the E28 and E34 editions of the M5, the Motorsport saloon based on the 5 Series that stood one notch further up the BMW range than the M3.**

So it was that when BMW management decided to put substantial money into a project to develop a mid-engined coupé that could beat the Porsche 911s in Group 5 track events, the Motorsport division was given the job of designing and developing it. The rules applied by the sport's governing body, FISA (the Fédération Internationale du Sport Automobile, or International Federation of Motor Sport), then insisted that no car could race unless it had been 'homologated' by production of a minimum number for sale to the public. So the new mid-engined coupé was developed with a dual purpose – to win on the tracks and to attract wealthy customers who wanted a race-bred supercar as their everyday transport.

The project to develop the car that became known as the M1 ran into all kinds of difficulties that do not need to be discussed in detail here. Briefly, the Motorsport division had no room to build the necessary 400 examples, and so the job was farmed out to Lamborghini in Italy and to Giugiaro's ItalDesign company, who had designed the body. This arrangement collapsed and BMW eventually called on German specialist Baur in Stuttgart to assemble the cars, but the delays meant that the M1 arrived late.

Worse, by the time it appeared, the racing regulations had been changed. The car was hastily transferred to the Group 6 category, and failed to qualify. Only a stroke of genius, cooked up between BMW's Jochen Neerpasch and Max Mosley, a leading light in the Formula One Constructors' Association (FOCA), got it onto the tracks at all. Between them, these two developed and implemented the Procar series, in which celebrity drivers would race M1s in special events to warm up the crowds before some of the European Grands Prix in 1979 and 1980.

Though the story of the M1 is in many ways a sad one, the car did have a very important influence over what came next. It drew the attention of a much wider public to the Motorsport brand, and this paved the way for BMW to sanction Motorsport editions of some of its other production models. Unlike the M1, these were not specially developed as complete cars. Instead, they would be versions of existing models that had been re-engineered to give more road performance.

The first of these cars was very much a cosmetic exercise, and was based on the most powerful version of the then-current E12 5 Series saloons. The M535i added a bodykit and

Regular upgrades have always added to the appeal of the cars from BMW M. These two are later versions of the E34 M5, with the 3.8-litre engine instead of the original 3.5-litre type. As the estate (or 'Touring') model makes clear, the M badge was not incompatible with everyday practicality – and that became one of the brand's great strengths.

other minor changes to the existing 535i model to give the basic car a more sporting focus, and was introduced in 1979 when the M1 was still new and exciting. Most importantly, it borrowed that same letter M as part of its name.

Four years later, BMW repeated the trick with a Motorsport version of the big 6 Series coupé. This time, though, it added genuine high performance to the mix. Badged as an M635 CSi, the new car combined the 4-valve, 3.5-litre engine of the M1 with a number of special features to create a new top-of-the-range Autobahn express. Like the M535i before it, the car was always built on the main BMW assembly lines in Munich, but it had the aura of a Motorsport car – and it

was certainly not lacking in performance. BMW quoted 6.4 seconds for the 0–60mph dash, and some magazine testers achieved even better than that.

The reaction to these M-badged cars made it quite clear to BMW that they had uncovered a new and potentially very profitable market. So 1983 became a critical year for the whole future of the Motorsport division. BMW decided that its interests would be best served by having the Motorsport engineers develop a range of high-performance cars with exclusive cosmetic details that would be derivatives of existing production models. This strategy would serve a number of purposes: first, it would minimize the cost of developing

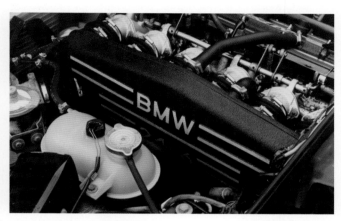

Attention to detail has also been a characteristic of the cars from BMW M. The finish on these 6-cylinder engines – clearly but not ostentatiously branded as coming from the Motorsport division – is simply beautiful.

these flagship models, which would have a 'halo' effect on the standard production cars and should help to increase sales; second, it would strengthen the BMW brand and particularly its association with high performance; and third, it would give BMW a series of products that its competitors would be unable to match in the short term.

That strategy has proved enormously successful over the years, but in the beginning it had to be backed up by some changes. Quite obviously, the Motorsport division was not going to be able to function efficiently if it was left skulking in some corner of the main factory at Munich. So a plan was drawn up to move the division into its own dedicated premises that would include offices, workshops and an assembly hall. A site was found in Garching to the east of Munich, at Daimlerstrasse (ironically named after Gottlieb Daimler, joint founder of BMW's great rival Daimler-Benz), and by 1986 it was ready. In the meantime, the marketing strategy was outlined and the model-naming strategy was modified. In future, there would be no more complicated names like M535i and M635 CSi. Instead, the Motorsport derivatives would use the numeral of the series on which they were based, preceded by the letter M.

This new and brilliantly simple naming strategy was unveiled in February 1984, when BMW revealed their new M5 model at the Amsterdam Motor Show. Based of course on the then-current E28 5 Series, it had another version of the M88 3.5-litre engine originally developed for the M1, plus an uprated 'chassis' and both trim and cosmetic changes that emphasized its no-nonsense sporting character. It was a sensation: here, straight out of the box, was the world's fastest regular-production four-door saloon. Suddenly, a lot of people realized that this was what they had wanted to own all along.

In fact, the first E28 M5s were built on the main assembly lines in Munich, but production transferred to Garching as soon as the new plant was ready in 1986. The new numbering system spread quickly: US-model M635 CSi cars were given an M6 badge, and in 1985 BMW announced that there would also be a Motorsport version of their two-door E30 3 Series cars. The full story behind the first M3 is told in Chapter 2 of this book, but that original M3 was the first of a line that lasted for more than a quarter of a century and became an icon for countless enthusiasts of high-performance cars.

THE M3 FAMILY: E30 AND E36

Undeniably, the M3 has had to move with the times, just as

the whole Motorsport division has had to adjust its activities and products to suit the demands of the market. What is easy to forget is that even if the Motorsport division is run by committed enthusiasts, the cars that are eventually released onto the market are the result of reasoned (maybe sometimes heated) debates between engineers and marketing specialists. BMW is in business to make money, after all.

The M3 made the glamour and performance of the Motorsport cars more affordable and quickly became the benchmark for every high-performance compact saloon. But that original M3 had a character that was quite different from that of the later cars to bear its name. It was a much more raw, hard-edged car, much more obviously designed for success on the racetracks than its descendants. It was this 'race car in civilian clothing' element that gave the car much of its initial appeal.

However, as a limited-production model, the original M3 was inevitably going to be expensive, and people who spend a lot of money on their cars expect better levels of comfort and equipment than are found in the typical track car. They want leather upholstery, electric windows, air conditioning and a whole host of other features that add weight and make the car less suitable for track use while making it more viable as everyday transport. So the first M3 – like its bigger brother the M5 – was offered with such features available as optional extras from the beginning.

Over the five years that the E30 M3 was on sale, BMW were taking very careful note of what the model's customers wanted. The introduction of a convertible derivative – the very antithesis of what a track car is all about – was made very early in the M3's production run, and in the later 1980s a number of special-edition models carefully tested public acceptance of new features, all the while giving customers the exclusivity they wanted because they were constructed in strictly limited numbers. So by the time the second-generation M3 models were ready to be launched, BMW knew exactly what it was doing. The M3 was, and always would be, an extremely well-made high-performance model with the special appeal of exclusivity, but it would also incorporate elements expected in a luxury car unless these conflicted with its high-performance, sharp-handling nature.

Some people argue that the E36 M3 that followed in 1992 was biased too far towards the 'exclusive' and 'luxury' elements of the M3 specification. Not that it was in any way lacking in performance – a smooth 6-cylinder engine that delivered extraordinary acceleration saw to that – but the very smoothness of that engine removed the rawness that

Excellence on the track was always an important element in the M3's make-up, and **BMW** celebrated forty years of its **M** division in 2012 by getting these four cars together. The then-current E90 series car is on the left, the blue car is an E46, the yellow car is an E36 and the red car on the right is the 4-cylinder E30 that started it all.

had been at the heart of the original M3's exciting nature. BMW had also chosen to spread the M3 formula more widely: there was now a four-door saloon in the 3 Series range, and so the car was available in three guises – coupé, convertible and saloon. The only body derivative of the E36 3 Series that was never sold with M3 badges was the Touring model, or estate car. Commentators also noted the change in the name of the M3's parent division: in 1993 it changed from BMW Motorsport to BMW M.

Yet this was certainly not an indication that BMW planned to lose sight of the M3's motor sport connections. Rather was it a prelude to a new and wider range of responsibilities within BMW as a whole for the division that had started out with a brief that only covered motor sport. The E36 M3s continued to appear in European touring car and GT events through the mid-1990s although their progress was hampered by rule changes, which led to a focus on smaller-engined cars. BMW North America ran a high-profile campaign on the tracks in the USA and, as Chapter 5 shows,

almost every special-edition derivative of the model had a direct link with motor sport. BMW was well aware that there were privateers who campaigned these cars at club level and other national events, and that their appearances on the tracks were good and cost-free publicity.

Very noticeable about the E36 era was that BMW were trying out new ideas, to see what M3 buyers would accept. Adding a four-door saloon to the range was just one part of this, and the company showed a willingness to try other new things. This was one reason why many of the special-edition models were market-specific: they were designed to see how different markets around the world reacted to certain elements in the M3's specification. But perhaps the most obvious change to the original M3 formula was the introduction of an automatic-transmission car for the USA in early 1995. The very idea of an automatic gearbox in a sporting car was complete anathema to driving enthusiasts in the days before advanced electronics could produce lightning-fast gearshifts that no human could match, but BMW knew

A CHANGE OF NAME

BMW Motorsport GmbH changed its name to BMW M GmbH in 1993, at just about the time the new E36 M3 models were coming on-stream.

There were several business reasons for the change, but one was undoubtedly the strength of the M brand. Another was that BMW had longer-term plans to give the M division a wider remit. In future, it would be responsible not only for motor sport activities but also for much of the bespoke work on production vehicles – including, of course, the M3 itself.

that American buyers were devoted to such things. They therefore gave them what they wanted, even if (as Chapter 4 shows) they had to compromise the essence of the M3 to a degree in order to achieve that.

It was just a temporary compromise, though. The Motorsport division was already working on a solution that would deliver two-pedal control without the power losses inherent in an automatic transmission dependent on a torque converter. Using racing technology, they developed what they called a Sequential Manual Gearbox, or SMG for short, which depended on a servo-actuated clutch and an electronic control system. Early versions of the SMG, introduced in 1996, tended to be somewhat troublesome, but BMW persevered with the technology and improved it to the point where an SMG-equipped car would actually accelerate faster than a conventional manual-gearbox model. By the time of the third-generation or E46 M3, there was no longer any need for an automatic gearbox in the range. The SMG did it all – and better.

THE M3 FAMILY: E46 AND THE E90-SERIES

The strength of the M brand and the marketing associated with the models from BMW's Motorsport division make it easy to misunderstand how the M models are developed. In the beginning, it was largely true that the Motorsport engineers were let loose on a mainstream BMW model after it had been readied for production, so that they were then

obliged to do a certain amount of re-engineering to make the car perform the way they wanted. But from the time of the E36, the Motorsport engineers were actually involved in the design process at an early stage, so that their likely requirements could be taken into account. This meant that far less re-engineering was necessary in order to turn a new BMW model into a Motorsport product. Suspension and braking components might be changed, and strengthening gussets might be welded in to stiffen a bodyshell, but essentially there would be far fewer compromises.

By the time of the third-generation M3, the process was well established. This third generation – actually the fourth generation of the BMW 3 Series – was the E46 that arrived in 2000. There would once again be coupé and convertible derivatives, but this time there would be no saloons. These had been the weakest sellers of the E36 range, and the Motorsport division had decided not to bother with a four-door M3 in the new range. Nevertheless, the E46 marked a step change in the history of the M3, because it was drawn up around the idea of a 'world' specification – one where the core specification needed few or no differences between one market and the next.

Once again, the move in that direction had begun with the E36, when BMW had made the first steps towards eliminating an automatic transmission from the options list by developing its SMG for customers who wanted two-pedal control. For the E46, the plan was to avoid using a traditional automatic gearbox at all, and so to remove the need for a low-revving version of the M3 engine that would work with proprietary automatics. SMG gave way to Dual-Clutch Transmission (DCT) that did the same job more efficiently.

With a little juggling of specifications, it proved possible to use essentially the same 6-cylinder engine for all world markets. The only significant variation was (as always) for the USA, which was using different emissions certification test procedures from other countries. However, BMW managed to incorporate the US-specific features within the catalytic converters, and this almost eliminated the extra manufacturing costs associated with having two very different versions of the engine in production. From the buyers' point of view, it also meant that the USA was not offered an excessively 'watered-down' version of the M3.

The link with motor sport was perhaps even more tenuous for this generation of M3, however. Despite an extra-cost Competition Package, which became available in all markets and would turn a standard M3 coupé (but not a convertible) into a credible track-day car, the E46 M3 was not widely perceived as a competition machine. Partly as a way of remedying this, BMW did make a hard-edged, lightweight special model called the M3 CSL for Europe. The USA, which was the M3's best market, was denied this, but not for want of trying. Before the CSL arrived, much of the lightweight specification had been tested on a very special racing M3 for the American Le Mans series (ALMS), and the plan had been to create a special edition on the back of this.

In practice, the special lightweight edition for the USA did not come to fruition: the project foundered on homologation rules, and BMW management decided it was all going to be too much expense and too much trouble. But the M3 GTR, as the car was called, did highlight a significant change in thinking from the Motorsport division. Seeking extra power, the Motorsport engineers had abandoned their silky-smooth 6-cylinder engine and had instead developed a hugely powerful version of the production V8 engine that was then used in the mainstream 5 Series.

What nobody knew at the time was that the next generation of M3 was in fact also slated to use a V8 engine, even though it would not be this one. The next generation of M5 saloon, due in 2005, was going to have a V10 engine related to the BMW race engine used in the 2004-season Williams FW26 Formula 1 car, and that left the way clear for the M3 to gain an extra pair of cylinders. Buyers would bemoan the disappearance of the M3's much-liked small-block 6-cylinder, but there was far more development potential in BMW's all-alloy V8 designs, and the Motorsport division was determined to exploit it.

The fourth generation of M3 was announced in 2006, a year after the first mainstream models of the new 3 Series had been introduced. This time, as Chapter 8 explains, BMW had developed saloon, estate, coupé and convertible as separate but related projects, and so there were four project codes for the cars. Nevertheless, the M3 would use only three of the available body shells, these being the E90 Saloon (the four-door car returned to the range), E92 Coupé and E93 Convertible. For the sake of simplicity, this book refers to them as the E90-series cars.

As we shall see in Chapter 9, BMW made strenuous efforts to re-establish the M3's competition links with the E90-series models. Every one of the special editions that followed over the next seven years had some connection – albeit sometimes rather tenuous – with motor sport. Even more important, though, was that BMW also campaigned M3-derived models in the ALMS series from 2009 and then from 2012 in the Deutsche Tourenwagen Meisterschaft

(DTM or German Touring Car Championship), where they were convinced that a 'silhouette' version of the M3 stood a good chance of winning against domestic rivals Mercedes-Benz and Audi. Their faith was not misplaced, either. The DTM M3s won BMW the manufacturers' title in 2012 as well as taking driver Bruno Spengler to the individual title. It looked as if the M3 had returned with a vengeance.

This success on the race tracks drew plenty of praise and no doubt did a power of good for the M3's image among buyers as well, but enthusiasts who looked into things a little more closely recognized that the 'silhouette' cars pounding the race tracks had only the barest of resemblances to the production M3s that they were able to buy. Those cars – and even the 2013 DTM Champion Edition that commemorated the 2012 win – were still primarily high-performance, prestigious luxury cars, designed more for those with plenty of money to spend than for those who remembered what the original M3 of 1986 had represented.

It is easy to be cynical, especially when evaluating an icon, but it was journalist Richard Meaden who had the courage to point out in print what many enthusiasts were thinking. In the August 2007 issue of *Evo* magazine, he wrote:

> *There's something of the ageing supergroup about the BMW M3. Celebrated some two decades ago for its groundbreaking purity and purpose, the M3's cult appeal has become something altogether different: a vastly lucrative franchise that enjoys growing sales with every subsequent release.*

Identification has been constant since the beginning. The badge on this BMW M1 from the end of the 1970s has a clear family resemblance to the badges used on all four generations of M3.

He went on to accept that:

whatever your viewpoint there's something undeniably awesome about the 21-year progression from delicate 2-litre, 4-cylinder, 200bhp road-racer to 4-litre, 8-cylinder, 414bhp monster. Few models have gone through such a total transformation, yet the M3 badge's power to provoke fevered pre-launch speculation and post-launch scrutiny remains as strong as ever.

The cat, though, was well and truly out of the bag, and the succession of depressingly similar special edition models that characterized the last few years of E90-series M3 production made it abundantly clear to many enthusiasts that the M3 name was perhaps losing some of its lustre.

It may be that BMW had been thinking along similar lines. Certainly, it let the world know some time before the M3's replacement was due that the new model would not bear the famous badge. Two-door derivatives of the 3 Series replacement would have 4 Series badges, and therefore the replacement for the M3 coupé and convertible, core models of the M3 range, would be badged as M4 models when they arrived in 2014. That in turn caused an outcry among M3 loyalists, which simply demonstrated the truth of the old adage that it is impossible to please all of the people all of the time.

AN EPITAPH

One way or another, the M3 name has had a very good run. As the rest of this book sets out to show, it has been applied to some extremely high-quality and hugely enjoyable cars that have set the standard for others in their class. Indeed, there have been times when there has been no class as such; the M3 has stood alone. Only in recent years have BMW's rivals really caught up – Mercedes-Benz with its AMG-branded models, Audi with its S cars, Jaguar with its R models, and Lexus with its F and F Sport models. Yet not one of these makers builds performance derivatives of its mainstream cars that enjoy a brand image comparable to that of the BMW M cars.

THE MOTORSPORT STORY AND THE M3 – SOME KEY DATES

1972	BMW Motorsport GmbH set up as a separate company to oversee all BMW competition activity.
1978	First complete car from the Motorsport division announced. The M1 is a mid-engined supercar, intended for the track and also built as a 'homologation special' for public sale.
1979	M535i becomes the first volume-production Motorsport derivative of a mainstream production BMW.
1983	M635 CSi introduced, with the 4-valve Motorsport engine from the M1.
1984	E28 M5, the first of the proper M-cars from BMW, is announced with the 4-valve engine from the M1.
1985	Announcement of the first M3, based on the E30 3 Series cars, and available from 1986. Its S14 engine is a distant relative of the E10, introduced in 1961.
1986	BMW Motorsport gets its own dedicated factory at Garching.
1987	M3 range expanded to include a convertible derivative.
1992	Introduction of the second-generation M3, based on the E36 3 Series and featuring a 6-cylinder engine. The initial coupé is followed in 1994 by convertible and saloon derivatives.
1995	US market receives an M3 with automatic transmission.
1996	Introduction of the SMG gearbox, giving two-pedal control with the selectability of a manual gearbox.
2000	Introduction of the third-generation M3, based on the E46 3 Series. Convertible versions follow in 2001, but there are no saloons.
2006	Introduction of the fourth-generation M3 as an E90 saloon, E92 coupé and an E93 convertible. New M-DCT transmission gives two-pedal control from 2008.
2012	BMW victorious in the DTM with the M3 'silhouette' based on the E92 coupé.
2013	Last E90-series M3 models built.

CHAPTER TWO

THE E30 M3

The origins of the first-generation M3 are rooted in the rivalry between BMW and Mercedes-Benz. Central to the BMW appeal was an element of sportiness that was not present in the cars manufactured by the Stuttgart company and, although Mercedes certainly had an illustrious competition history, it generally focused on other qualities to promote its cars in the 1970s and 1980s.

What changed all that was the success of the original BMW 3 Series, the E21 range introduced in 1975. Compact, affordable and sporty, it set a new standard for cars of its size, and Mercedes-Benz realized that they too would have to develop a car in that class if they were to maintain their leadership of the German car industry. So the late 1970s saw the Stuttgart company working on their new W201 model, which would be announced in 1982 as the 190.

To make it different from the small BMW, Mercedes decided to produce their 190 only as a four-door car, and to give it the right sort of image they decided to develop a racing version eligible for the European touring car championships. Some time before the 190 actually entered production, BMW got wind of what was going on. One result was that they developed the second-generation 3 Series car,

called E30, in both two-door and four-door versions (and in estate and convertible forms as well) to make sure they had maximum coverage of the potential market.

The other main result was that they started work on a high-performance E30 that they could take racing and with which they hoped to beat Mercedes at their own game. Nevertheless, they were caught wrong-footed in the beginning. The road-going version of the racing Mercedes, called a 190E 2.3-16 and featuring a 4-valve engine developed with the aid of Cosworth Engineering in the UK, was announced a full two years before BMW got the M3 into production. As *What Car?* magazine suggested in October 1986, for a company whose 'whole marketing philosophy has been centred around the performance aspects of its cars, [that] must... have been a slap in the face.'

It looks as if BMW started work on the E30 M3 in 1981, a year before the E30 and the new small Mercedes entered production in a head-on clash. The first task was to create an engine suitable for racing, and in fact the whole M3 project was undertaken from the same perspective: design an E30-based car that would be competitive in Group A touring car races, and then make a road-going derivative that

As introduced, the E30 3 Series was a two-door saloon. Only later did four-door and convertible models appear, and the original M3 was based on the standard two-door saloon variant. Comparing the standard E30 (left) with the M3 (right) makes clear just what the Motorsport division did to the car – and how very nearly outrageous the M3 appeared in the mid-1980s.

would sell the 5,000 examples necessary to obtain racing homologation under the FISA rules.

THE ENGINE

By the time that the idea of a high-performance E30 derivative surfaced, the direction of BMW engine development was already clear. The idea of turbocharging, tried on the legendary 2002 turbo of 1973, had been abandoned when that car had proved somewhat challenging to drive in its road-going form. All the focus was now on 4-valve cylinder heads. There was already a 4-valve head on the 4-cylinder Formula 2 racing engines that the Motorsport division was building, and there was a 4-valve head on the 3.5-litre, 6-cylinder, twin-cam engine used in the M1 and the M635 CSi, and planned for the 1985 M5.

One faction within BMW favoured transplanting the 6-cylinder engine straight into the E30 to create the high-performance car. This demanded major surgery at the front end of the bodyshell, but it was achievable, and it seems that

a single prototype was actually built to test the idea. However, there was no doubt that the weight of the big 6-cylinder engine affected the car's handling and that expensive major development work would therefore be necessary.

So attention switched to a 4-valve development of the existing 2.0-litre M10 4-cylinder engine. This would be lighter, which would reduce the need for suspension development; it would help differentiate the road-going car from the new M5 model, which had the 4-valve, 6-cylinder engine; and it would

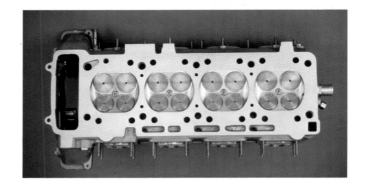

The engine in the E30 M3 was a 4-cylinder, ultimately derived from the great M10 4-cylinder that had been key to BMW's revival in the 1960s. Its key feature was the 4-valve head, derived from racing practice.

be cheaper, which would make the car more saleable as a road vehicle. This was an important factor because before the E30 could be homologated (approved for racing) in Group A touring car events, FISA rules required that 5,000 road-going examples had to be built for sale in a period of just 12 months.

The man behind all the 4-valve BMW engines at the time was Paul Rosche, and his team assembled the first prototype of the new 4-cylinder engine over the summer of 1981. The cylinder block was essentially that of the 2.0-litre M10 production engine but reinforced and bored out to the same 93.4mm dimension that was used in the 6-cylinders. This gave the necessary space for the four valves, and a special crankshaft that gave the same 84mm stroke as the 6-cylinders meant that time could be saved by using their proven combustion-chamber design. Cast pistons reduced weight, and the prototype engine was completed with the aid of a cut-and-shut cylinder head from one of the production 4-valve sixes.

Straightaway the results were excellent, and so the engine was immediately handed over to a development team headed by Werner Frowein. Detail work over the next year or so resulted in an engine that delivered 200PS at 6,750rpm with 239Nm (176lb ft) at 4,750rpm in road trim, and offered the potential for around 50 per cent more power in Group A racing form. At this stage, however, no work had been done on catalytic converters; BMW knew that this would limit sales of the high-performance E30 to Europe, but were prepared to accept that success in European touring car racing would have little impact on sales in the two big 'cat' markets of the USA and Japan.

That all changed under the impact of German politics. Driven largely by the Green Party, which was gradually gain-

ing influence in the early 1980s, the West German government announced that it would begin to regulate exhaust emissions from the mid-1980s. The issue at stake was acid rain and its effect on the country's forests, and it gave rise to heated debates at the time. Nevertheless, the government developed an incentives plan that would begin in mid-1985. They advised car makers to offer catalytic converters on new cars from July that year, and in return exempted cars so equipped from taxation for a fixed period; on engines larger than 2.0 litres that period would run to the end of 1987. At the same time, they reduced tax on the unleaded petrol that was necessary for cars with catalytic converters, and raised tax on leaded petrol by a corresponding amount. From the start of 1986, road tax would increase by 50 per cent for cars that could not use unleaded petrol.

All this left BMW with no choice. If they could not offer a catalyst-equipped version of their new high-performance E30 for their own home market, it would take very much longer to sell the necessary 5,000 examples. So the Motorsport division embarked on a crash programme to develop the catalyst-equipped engine. It all took time and cost money, but an advantage was that the car would now be saleable in the USA and Japan as well as in Europe. By the time the new engine was signed off for production, the version with twin in-line catalytic converters was producing 195PS and 229Nm (169lb ft) – figures remarkably close to those of the non-cat engine at a time when catalytic converters typically absorbed depressingly high amounts of engine power.

DEVELOPING THE CAR

Meanwhile, development began on the car itself early in

Right first time – or almost. This is a design mock-up for the first M3, pictured in November 1984. The lines are right, but the bulging wings look too much like add-ons. The lines of the door would be continued across both front and rear wings on production cars.

This side view of an early production car shows how the lines were modified to give a more unified appearance.

ABOVE AND LEFT: **The dashboard and controls of the E30 M3 were essentially those of the standard E30 saloon, but both the lower spoke of the steering wheel and the gear shift grip carried the Motorsport colours. There were no concessions to overseas markets, and the controls of the on-board computer were all labelled in German.**

1983. The E30 was already in volume production, having been announced at the Frankfurt Motor Show in September 1982. At BMW Motorsport GmbH, the M3 project was entrusted to Thomas Ammerschläger, who had gained a formidable reputation for his work on the Zakspeed Ford Capris and then on the original Audi Quattro.

There was never any question that the M3 should be based on the two-door E30 body rather than the four-door; it was lighter, and weight counts in racing. However, as development proceeded, so the M3 shell began to differ more and more from the standard production type. Some quite fundamental alterations were needed to accommodate the rollover cage required for racing, while flared wings were needed to take the wider 10-inch wheels that would be needed on the tracks. Then a 70-litre fuel tank was squeezed in to take the place of the standard 55-litre type; this car was going to be thirstier than the standard models, and extra fuel can also help in competition.

Aerodynamics also had a big impact. The profile was changed by raising the line of the boot lid by around 40mm (1.5in), and the rake of the rear window was altered to help deflect airflow towards a wing-type spoiler mounted on that boot lid. A deep front air dam was added to manage airflow around and under the car, and even the side sills were reshaped to help. In the end, of the outer panels only the bonnet and roof were shared with the standard production E30, and the car's Cd improved from the standard 0.36 to a creditable 0.33.

Though the special flared wings were made of steel, the other special outer panels – front bumper and apron, side sills, C-pillar covers, boot lid and rear spoiler, rear bumper and apron – were made of SMC plastic. The front- and rear-bumper mouldings concealed bumpers that met the US Federal 2.5mph (4km/h) impact requirement, and these were made standard for all E30 M3 models. For additional body rigidity, the front and rear screens were bonded to the bodyshell rather than rubber-glazed as on standard E30s.

The result of all these visual changes – designed, of course, for practical reasons and not for effect – was to make the M3 look splendidly aggressive. One story has it that BMW management had a fit of nerves when they saw it; the Greens had objected that the 2002 turbo looked aggressive some years earlier, and nobody wanted a repeat of that episode.

The fuel-saving overdrive fifth gear that was used on the standard E30s was not going to be needed for the M3. So the development team settled on a trusted close-ratio gearbox made by Getrag (who also supplied the production gear-

The M3 had a special rear window fairing and a special boot lid.

boxes). This also had five speeds, but with a direct top, and it came with a dog-leg first gear, selected by shifting the lever to the left of the main H-gate and then forwards. The torque of the engine allowed tall final-drive gearing for high maximum speeds, and a ZF 25 per cent limited-slip differential was chosen to improve traction under power. Not surprisingly, a special bonded clutch lining also found its way into the specification.

The suspension of the standard E30 had been carefully tuned to give the optimum compromise between ride comfort and handling, but the M3 development team had no such constraints. Their priority was to get the best possible handling from the car for racing; the suspension could

The suspension of the E30 M3 was straightforward by later standards, as these pictures of a display 'chassis' show. It had nevertheless been altered from the standard E30 set-up.

always be tweaked a little to give better comfort for the road versions. So they altered the front strut geometry to give more castor for better stability, and relocated the anti-roll bar so that it was attached to the struts rather than to the control arms, as on the standard E30. The rear anti-roll bar was made thicker, and the angle of the trailing arms was changed (to 15 degrees), while stiffer springs were fitted. Twin-tube Boge gas dampers were specified all round, and shorter springs front and rear dropped the ride height by around an inch (25mm).

For the braking system, the Motorsport team turned to existing production models, taking the essential elements from the E28 5 Series saloons. From the 535i came 280mm (11in) ventilated front discs, with 282mm (11.1in) solid discs at the rear. ABS was of course to be made standard, and

it was simply a question of tuning the system to suit the car. The E28 5 Series parts bin was also plundered for the stub axles, which brought not only larger wheel bearings than on the standard E30s but also five-stud wheel hubs. As a result, the M3 became the only E30 variant to have five-stud wheels; all the others had four-stud types. This in turn demanded a new design of wheel, and for production cars BMW turned to BBS, who provided an attractive multi-spoke design with a 7-inch rim. The racers, of course, would have much wider rims.

As for the steering, a quicker-than-standard rack gave 3.6 turns of the wheel from lock to lock compared with the standard E30's 4.5 turns. A decision was also taken that there would be no cars with right-hand drive. This was part-ly to save development time and costs: the racers would be fine with left-hand drive and BMW's view was that relatively few sales would be made in RHD markets anyway. Another issue, however, was that engineering a RHD version would require a redesign of the exhaust manifold in order to clear a RHD steering rack. The engineers had calculated that this was likely to rob the engine of around 10PS, and this very much counted against even trying.

The interior of the cabin was designed to rather different criteria: for a Group A touring car, issues such as the upholstery colour are rather less important than whether the rev counter is easily visible. The road cars were therefore kitted out with an eye to attracting buyers. Essentially, their interiors were based on those of the standard E30s, but with a few special features. The Recaro 'bucket' seats optional on other E30s were made standard, while there was a special contoured rear seat for two. A black headlining gave a unique interior ambience, to which red instrument needles added a

ABOVE AND BELOW: **The shape and upholstery of the Recaro front bucket seats was special to the M3. The rear seats were upholstered to match in grey, with a houndstooth check for the centre panels.**

little drama. An 8,000rpm rev counter and special 260km/h speedometer (or a 160mph type for markets that needed it) were necessary features, as was an oil-temperature gauge in place of the standard econometer. A three-spoke M-Technic I steering wheel with Motorsport tricolour stripe on the centre spoke gave a sporty feel, and the whole was set off by a small M logo between the main dials.

As always happens in a car intended for multiple markets, a variety of optional features was prepared. Nevertheless, the car was presented as a stripped-down competition machine, even if it did come with tinted glass and electric door mirrors as standard. Options – standard in some markets – included leather upholstery, heated seats, rear head restraints, metallic paint, air conditioning, an on-board computer, electric windows, an electric sunroof, a headlamp wash-wipe system and of course a variety of ICE systems. There was the option of larger wheels and tyres, too, with low-profile tyres on 16-inch wheels with 7.5-inch rims an alternative to the standard 15-inch type with 7-inch rims.

The badge on the rear was simple but effective, combining the 3 from the 3 Series designation with the M of the Motorsport division.

THE FIRST CARS

BMW Motorsport had a pre-production car ready in time for the Frankfurt Motor Show in September 1985, and proudly displayed it there as a statement of intent. Everybody knew, though, that BMW were playing catch-up at this stage: the rival Mercedes-Benz 190E 2.3-16 had been announced more than a year earlier. Of interest was that the new high-performance E30 was introduced with the name of M3. Earlier model names from the Motorsport division had been more than a little confused – the M1 had been followed by the M535i and M635 CSi, for example – but it now looked as if a pattern was emerging. The high-performance derivative of the 5 Series introduced at the Amsterdam Motor Show in 1984 had been simply called an M5. The new E30 derivative followed that lead.

In fact, volume production was still a year away when the M3 was announced. The first 'production' cars were assembled in March 1986, but full volume was not achieved until September 1986. By this stage, the European media had already been able to sample the M3 at a ride-and-drive exercise held at the Mugello circuit near Florence in Italy during May. As the Motorsport plant in Garching did not have the capacity for the volumes needed, the M3 was batch-produced on the main BMW assembly lines in the Munich suburb of Milbertshofen. Dedicated teams worked

alongside the lines on the sub-assemblies unique to the car, and then these were built into the body shells on the moving production line.

BMW's top priority was to build the 5,000 customer cars needed for Group A homologation as quickly as possible, and they managed to achieve this by 1 March 1987, 12 months from the start of production. What that did was to distort the production figures quite markedly, so that they suggest interest in the M3 dropped off sharply from 1988. In fact, all that had happened was that production had settled down to a volume more suited to the tempo of sales. In the beginning, cars must have been stockpiled while the dealers did their best to move them through the showrooms.

As these early sales were made, however, it must have quickly become apparent that BMW had something much more exciting on their hands than they had expected. The M3 was attracting customers beyond the obvious hard core of enthusiasts: it was becoming a status symbol among those who would never go anywhere near a racing circuit. So the obvious thing to do was to exploit that interest; BMW is of course in business to make money, and not just to build exotic machines for niche customers. The next stage, then, was to see how the M3 could be developed as a range of cars.

THE FIRST EVOLUTION

Meanwhile, BMW was already looking at the next stage in the M3's racing career. To keep the model competitive on the tracks, they were going to need to make some changes, and of course FISA regulations dictated how they were able to do that. A minimum of 500 production cars were required for each major design evolution of a homologated racing type, and BMW coped with that by building a special edition from February 1987, which they simply called the M3 Evolution. In practice, they built 505 examples, and production ended in May 1987.

The Evolution cars had a further-developed engine with a new cylinder head and other minor changes. The new head was distinguished by an E mark (for Evolution) below the inlet tract for number four cylinder, but power was still quoted at the 200PS of the standard engine; the changes made no difference to the production engine but did allow further power increases on the more highly-tuned Group A cars. Like the standard engine, the Evolution type did not have a catalytic converter.

Nevertheless, there were other, more noticeable differences compared with the standard cars. These were mainly associated with fine-tuning of the aerodynamics. The Evolution front air dam had a small spoiler extension at the bottom and had air ducts for the front brakes where the standard cars had fog lamps. The rear spoiler now had a small secondary lip under its main wing to improve high-speed handling on the racers (it was of course of no value in everyday motoring). Then there was some additional weight saving from a new lightweight boot lid.

Just seven of these cars were imported into the UK when they were new, although with the passage of time the total in the country may have changed.

THE 1988 M3

The M3's third season in production was a busy one. It saw the introduction of the car to North America and Japan – two markets not foreseen under the original scheme – and it saw the arrival of a second Evolution model and the introduction of a convertible derivative.

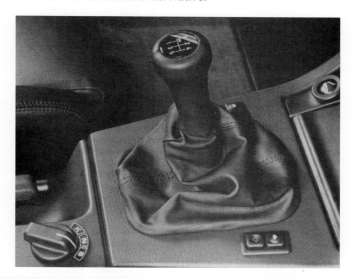

Clear in the first picture is the three-position Electronic Damper Control (EDC). Lights on the dashboard indicated the chosen setting to the driver. The Motorsport division's stripes are visible on the gearshift grip, which betrays the 'dog-leg' gate of the five-speed gearbox. Early grips had no gate pattern but only the M logo.

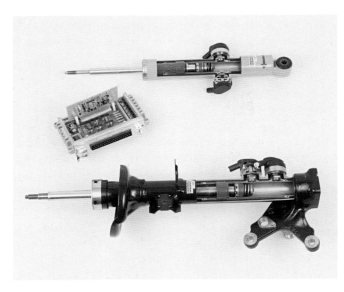

These are the electronically controlled dampers themselves, together with their control box.

There were some specification changes, too. From September 1987, all cars were fitted with new ellipsoid headlights that incorporated a sidelamp bulb. Then, from an indeterminate point in the new calendar year, Electronic Damper Control (EDC) was added to the options list for the European-specification cars. The system was made by Boge and was controlled from a rotary knob on the centre console. It offered three different damper settings, Normal (N),

The 5,000th M3 was built on 23 February 1987, and the end-of-line ceremony featured works drivers Marc Hessel, Roberto Ravaglia and Annette Meeuwissen.

Sport (S) and Comfort (K – the German word is *Komfort*), and incorporated an automatic override to the Sport setting during high-speed driving. Though the differences between one setting and another were hard to detect in everyday driving, the ultra-firm Sport setting did offer a little more control during spirited driving.

THE M3 FOR NORTH AMERICA

As the first of the Evolution cars were reaching European buyers, the M3 was launched in North America. Production began in March 1987, straight after those first 5,000 cars had been built, and the first 101 North American cars were built as 1987 models even though BMW North America marketed them as 1988 cars when they went on sale over the summer of 1987. The press ride-and-drive exercise was held at the Lime Rock Park racing circuit in Connecticut in June, and the cars reached showrooms shortly after that.

In most respects, the US version of the E30 M3 was identical to the standard (non-Evolution) European version, but there were a few differences to suit local regulations and local preferences. So the North American M3s had side marker lights in the bumpers, slightly different headlights, and a third brake light mounted on the parcel shelf behind the rear window. They also had black intake grilles near each front fog light, where European cars had body-coloured covers for the towing hooks. Metallic paint was an extra-cost option.

Interiors were notable for generally higher levels of equipment than on European cars – American buyers wanted their creature comforts. So all cars for North America came with Bison leather upholstery, air conditioning, cruise control, electric windows and sunroof, an on-board trip computer and a top-quality eight-speaker AM/FM stereo radio-cassette ICE system. Cars for the USA of course had miles-per-hour speedometers, although those for Canada had kilometres-per-hour instruments; the Canadian cars also had heated front seats from the beginning.

The engine was the European catalyst-equipped type, rated at 192bhp by the SAE standards familiar in the USA, but had a different air-intake arrangement. The gearbox, however, was very different. BMW North America had felt that their customers would not take to the dog-leg Getrag gearbox, and so the North American M3 had the five-speed 'sports' gearbox from the 325i model, also made by Getrag but with a more conventional H-gate for the first four gears,

THE E30 M3 IN JAPAN

Once the catalyst-equipped North American version of the E30 M3 had been developed, it was a relatively simple task to adapt the car for the Japanese market. The Japanese cars became available in July 1987 and, like the North American models, they had the 195PS catalyst-equipped engine and five-speed 'sports' gearbox with conventional shift gate.

Standard equipment included electric windows, air conditioning and an on-board computer. Leather upholstery and an electric sunroof were the only options available.

Production of the M3 for Japan ended in March 1989. A total of 395 cars had been built specifically for this market.

and fifth out on its own. The wider ratios of this gearbox were offset by a shorter final drive of 4.10:1.

When the 'true' 1988 models entered production in September 1987, they came with the latest ellipsoid headlamps and some different colour options. So Cinnabar Red (code 138) replaced the earlier Henna Red (052) for the bodywork. Inside, Silver leather (code 0292) was a new option, and Natur leather (0295) replaced Pearl Beige (0206). Otherwise, the model change was detectable only in the tenth

digit of the VIN code, where a J for 1988 replaced the H for 1987.

THE EVOLUTION II

For the 1988 racing season, BMW needed further major changes to their Group A cars, and so of course they homologated these by another special edition. Build of the M3 Evolution II began in March 1988 and ended in May after 500 cars had been constructed (although it appears that there were actually 501 examples). Confusingly, BMW often refer to this model simply as an M3 Evolution, because the company sees the 1987 Evolution model as a variation of the standard car and not as a separate edition.

The key change this time was to a 220PS engine. The 2.3-litre swept volume remained unchanged, and the extra power came from new camshafts and pistons that gave a higher (11:1) compression, a remapped engine-management system, a lightened flywheel and a new air-intake tube. For purely cosmetic reasons, the Evolution II engines had their cam covers and air-collector boxes enamelled in white, with the tricolour stripes of the Motorsport division. With a taller 3.15:1 final drive, the road car could now achieve a maximum of 245km/h (152mph) as against the standard car's 235km/h (146mph), while the 0–100km/h (0–62mph) sprint figure remained unchanged at 6.7 seconds.

This time, BMW had taken the trouble to make the limited-build car more distinctive from the standard M3.

This is a 1988 Evolution II in Nogaro Silver that was sold by UK specialist company Munich Legends. The special front spoiler improved aerodynamics on the race track, and the model's unique grey-check upholstery can be seen through the windows.

Brightly painted, this was the special finish on the Evolution II engine.

It was available in only three colours: Macao Blue, Misano Red and Nogaro Silver. The windscreen had a green-tinted top strip, and the optional 16-inch wheels with their 7.5-inch rims were standard. These rode on low-profile Pirelli 225/45ZR16 tyres. Interiors all came with a unique half-leather upholstery in Silver, and all four seats carried tri-colour M labels. There were M3-branded kick plates and an M footrest for the driver, and the centre console carried a numbered plaque showing each car's position within the limited-edition run.

There were other invisible improvements. Although the front and rear spoilers shared their design with the earlier Evolution model, they were made of lightweight material. So were the bumper supports and the boot lid, and further weight was saved by using lighter glass in the rear screen and side windows. The difference was around 10kg (22lb) as compared to a standard M3 saloon.

Originally, 51 of the 501 Evolution II models were imported to the UK through official channels.

Details count... in this case, the Motorsport tricolour emblem on the backrest of an Evolution II front seat.

It was only May 1988 when the 10,000th M3 was built. This picture was taken at the internal celebrations by a BMW employee.

THE M3 CONVERTIBLE

There were two obvious ways of broadening the M3 range and capitalizing on the original car's success. BMW had four different E30 bodyshells in production, and these were the two-door saloon, the four-door saloon, the four-door estate (known as the Touring) and the convertible. The M3 was already a two-door saloon, and there was little point in making a four-door saloon alternative because it would be too similar to the existing car. So investigations began into touring and convertible derivatives.

Public acceptance of the M3 as a prestige purchase gave BMW the green light to offer a convertible version. This came as standard with a power-operated roof that was operated from a switch on the centre console.

According to legend, a single M3 Touring prototype was built, and was capable of a maximum 241km/h (150mph). However, development was not continued. Far more attractive, at least to the Marketing Department, was a convertible version of the M3, and so development went ahead on that. The decision to go with a convertible was a very important one in the whole history of the M3. It marked the point at which the car ceased to be a homologation special and became a prestige product. A convertible M3 was simply not a realistic proposition for competition purposes – but it was a highly desirable car that combined the obvious attraction of the convertible E30 with the status that the M3 name had already acquired.

The convertible E30 had been developed at least partly to give BMW a model that Mercedes' rival 190 range did not have. A pre-production car was shown at Frankfurt in September 1985 – panelled to represent an M3 derivative although in fact it had a standard production 6-cylinder engine and four-wheel drive as well – and volume production began in January 1986. Based on the two-door shell, the convertible version was heavily reinforced to restore the torsional stiffness lost through the absence of a roof.

The side sills were stronger and had strengthening members inside; the floorpan was reinforced with thicker steel for the transmission tunnel and a double-skinned rear seat pan; and there was extra steel plate welded between the rear side panels and rear inner wings. More reinforcement was in the scuttle and under the dash, and there were stiffening panels in the front wheel arches. Then there were extra panels welded where the A-pillars met the side sills, and a bracing bar between the steering column and the transmission tunnel. There were still little tremors through the body on poor surfaces, but the standard E30 Convertible was largely devoid of the scuttle shake that normally blights open cars.

One of its best features was the superb soft top, which had been developed for BMW by Shaer Waechter in Düsseldorf. Its fabric was of triple-layer sandwich construction, with an outer layer of artificial fibres, a 'sandwich' layer of sound-deadening rubber and a cotton inner layer. The whole was supported on six transverse hood bars, and the frame further consisted of seven sticks on each side, all moving in Teflon-seated bearings to give a smooth action.

All this was turned into an M3 from May 1988 by equipping the standard Convertible bodyshell with the special M3 drivetrain and other features, although a pre-production car was shown at Frankfurt in September 1987. Build volumes were always low enough for the cars to be assembled by hand at the BMW Motorsport operation in Garching. Bodies were supplied from the E30 assembly lines and then fitted out at Garching with the M3 drivetrain, suspension and interior. The M3 convertibles took on the saloon's flared wings, special front spoiler and BBS wheels. However, the special boot lid and rear spoiler simply did not work with the convertible body, and so the car had the standard E30 boot lid with no spoiler.

Interior features were essentially the same as for the M3 saloon, although of course there was a special, narrower rear seat to fit between the panels that concealed the hood frame on either side. All Convertibles had electric windows and M3-branded kick plates, and when the optional leather upholstery was fitted it was always the 'extended' type, with leather on the centre console, door panels and door pulls. The door panels were a unique type with diagonal pleating, and leather seats always had M tricolour labels. And, as befitted its position of high-status car, the M3 Convertible was fitted as standard with a power-operated soft top, something that was not even optional on lesser E30 convertibles. Probably few customers complained that its fuel tank was (by necessity) smaller than that of the M3 saloon.

The Convertible's hand-built nature meant that it was possible to have special features built into the car to order (and at extra cost). Known examples included suede trim, leather dashboard covering and mobile phone wiring. There was also one very special (and very rare) option that was unique to the car, and that was a removable hardtop with electrically heated rear window.

The M3 Convertible was some 181kg (400 lb) heavier than the saloon, and rode on different springs and dampers as a result. It was also slightly slower, and there were those who criticized it as a car with a split personality. Less crisp than the saloon in its handling, it had all the outward show of a racing machine but much of the character of an expensive boulevardier. It also had all the character that might have appealed in California, but in fact there would never be any official North American M3 Convertibles.

The E30 M3 Convertible was available initially with the 200PS 'non-cat' engine and then from October 1988 with the 195PS catalyst-equipped engine. Just one car (with VIN EB 85020) was allegedly built with the 220PS engine of the Evolution II. The cars were assembled in three batches at Garching, and their production ran from June 1988 to September 1988, March 1989 to June 1989 and then March 1990 to June 1991.

This late example of
the M3 Convertible
photographed by
Nick Dimbleby
shows the Evo-style
front spoiler that
was standard wear.

THE 1989 MODELS

The Convertible's arrival late in the 1988 season meant that it served as the headliner for the 1989 model year that began in October 1988. So there were no other major changes for the 1989 model year – although BMW did lead off in Europe with the first-ever M3 special edition in October, called the Europameister 88 Celebration. Not content with that, BMW capitalized on their motor sport success with a second special edition in spring 1989, this time with different variants for different markets. This later special edition was also used to introduce a new 215PS engine that would later become standard.

For the USA, 1989-model production actually began in July 1988. The 1989 cars came with a new ICE system that had CD-changer capability. No CD changer was available before September, however, and then it was a factory-fitted, extra-cost option. The only other change was that the Cardinal Red interior colour option was deleted.

THE 1990 MODELS

Changes anticipating the 1990 model year began in June 1989, when aluminium control arms with new bushes replaced steel types in the front suspension. The last of the non-catalyst 200PS engines was built in July, and the new 215PS engine became standard in European M3s when the 1990 model year began properly in September.

The 1990 cars also took on a new standard steering wheel. This had a thicker rim than before, with the M logo on the hub, and was known as an M-Technic II type. Cars with a driver's airbag had a different wheel. A leather handbrake boot and leather gear lever boot also became standard, while a leather shift grip was used with both types of gearbox. This had a tricolour stripe, and was attached to the gear lever boot. All cars also took on a vehicle check control monitor, with its display mounted above the rear-view mirror.

Then from December 1989 there was yet another special homologation edition, this time called the Sport Evolution III. Meanwhile, the Swiss market was somewhat belatedly treated to its own version of the special editions made available elsewhere earlier in the year. Also worth noting is that there was a break in the production of the M3 Convertible between June 1989 and February 1990. Production resumed in March, when Convertibles followed the saloons in taking on the new 215PS engine.

Later M3 steering wheels had a small M logo in place of the tricolour stripes on the lower spoke.

In North America, however, the 1990 models brought some extra changes. Their production actually began a few months earlier than the 1990 European models, to counter delays in showroom availability caused by shipping times across the Atlantic. The 1990-model North American M3s had new halogen headlights instead of the earlier ellipsoid units, and their rear quarter-windows were now fixed in place – which was hardly an improvement. There were aluminium control arms instead of steel items, and these now had different bushes. Under the bonnet, the cars now had the larger air-intake box of the Europe-only Evolution II cars. The options list was expanded, too, and an electric glass sunroof ('moonroof' to Americans) became available, alongside the heated front seats that were already standard on Canadian-market cars.

As the European cars came on-stream in September, some further changes were made. New colours were introduced, reflecting the change on the production lines, and, uniquely for the USA, cars now came as standard with a driver's-side airbag and a padded knee bolster. Both airbag and bolster were made extra-cost options for Canada. Nevertheless, the North American cars never did get the new 215PS engine, and stayed with the 195PS catalyst-equipped type until the end.

THE SPORT EVOLUTION

To keep the M3 competitive on the racing circuits, BMW needed more power from a bigger engine. Mercedes-Benz

had gone to a 2.5-litre engine in 1988 for their 190E 2.5-16, and it was to 2.5 litres that BMW now enlarged the M3's engine. A larger bore and a longer stroke took the swept volume up to 2467cc, and peak power went up to 238PS in road tune (although of course the racing cars developed considerably more). While the compression ratio was actually lower, at 10.2:1, new camshafts gave a longer valve-opening time, the inlet valves were enlarged by 0.5mm (0.02in) to improve breathing, and the exhaust valves were now sodium-filled to help keep them cool. Meanwhile, additional oil jets were sprayed onto the pistons from below, again in the interests of cooling.

To enable this engine to take to the tracks, BMW put it into a limited run of 600 cars that were initially called Evolution III Sport types but subsequently became known as Sport Evolution models. That figure of 600 was interesting in itself: the FISA regulations demanded a run of 500 cars,

This Sport Evolution model shows how BMW had begun to understand the delight that its M3 customers took in small details. The dark wheel centres and contrasting red bumper stripes were exactly right for the market.

When the Sport Evolution came in Brilliant Red, black was used as the contrast colour on the bumpers. Clear here are the additional front spoiler extension, the dark-centred wheels, and the additional aerofoil on the rear spoiler. This was always finished in black.

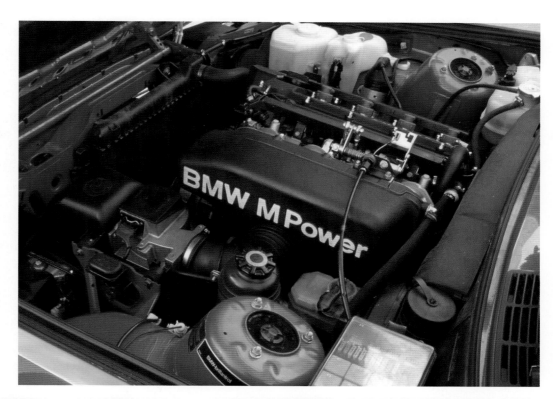

The engine in the Sport Evolution models was enlarged to 2.5 litres, and was surprisingly soberly finished – but note the red-spark plug covers! Perhaps reactions to the gaudy paint scheme of the Evolution II engine had discouraged BMW from further experiments in that direction.

but by this stage BMW knew very well that they could sell more than that. The cars were all built between December 1989 and March 1990.

The Sport Evolution came in just two colours, Brilliant Red with black bumper inserts or Jet Black with red bumper inserts. A similar effect was achieved under the bonnet, where the engine had a black cam cover with contrasting red spark-plug leads. From the outside, the Sport Evolution looked a lot like the Evolution II models from 1988 but

actually had fatter wheel arches to allow for even wider wheels on the racers. The road cars, though, had the familiar BBS wheels with 7.5-inch rims, shod this time with Michelin MXX 225/45ZR16 tyres and with their spokes painted in Nogaro Silver.

Distinguishing features were new adjustable spoilers at front and rear. Additional flaps under the front air dam and on top of the rear spoiler were attached by Allen screws and could be repositioned to alter the aerodynamics to suit different race circuits. Needless to say, they had no practical function on the road cars – although they were certainly a talking-point. The ride height had been lowered by 10mm (0.4in) all round, too.

Aerodynamic development had brought some other minor changes. A rubber strip now sealed the gap between each front wing and the bonnet, while rubber inserts around the headlamps and front-grille mountings blocked off more sources of airflow disturbance. Even the grille vanes had been re-profiled. More weight had been pared from the cars to counter the additional weight of the new engine, so the Sport Evolution had the smaller 62-litre (13.6-gallon) fuel tank from the 325i model, the thinner glass for side and rear windows, lightened front and rear bumpers, and neither map lights nor roof grab handles.

However, this was a road car and BMW knew by now what their customers wanted. So the interior had several additional 'surprise and delight' features: suede covers for the steering wheel rim, handbrake grip and illuminated shift grip; special sports seats with wraparound wings at shoulder height and slots for racing harnesses; red safety belts; a new striped pattern for the upholstery and door trims; and the M3-branded sill kick plates. A special plaque on the centre console carried the model identification and date of manufacture, but not (contrary to popular belief) a production number.

With the same 3.15:1 final drive as the Evolution II, the Sport Evolution models could reach 248km/h (154mph) and despatch the 0–100km/h (0–62mph) sprint in 6.5 seconds. A total of 45 were officially imported new into the UK, and *Performance Car* magazine tested one for their August 1990 issue. Perhaps their most telling comment was that 'The M3 is conspicuous even in yuppie West London'!

THE FINAL CARS

Under development since 1983, the E36 successor model to the E30 range was announced at the end of 1990, and there was no point in prolonging the life of the E30 M3 any further. So the 1991-season cars continued without change until December 1990, when the last saloons for all markets were built. As always, North American production began slightly before European production, in this case in June 1990.

Nevertheless, the final E30 M3 models to be completed were actually Convertibles, completed at the Motorsport plant in Garching as late as July 1991. They seem not to have lingered in the showrooms: even this late and with a new model eagerly expected, there were still buyers for this most glamorous of BMWs.

Although the M3 was a special derivative of the mainstream range, it was still a volume-produced car. These examples are going through end-of-line checks – although the photograph appears to have been specially posed.

COLOURS AND TRIMS FOR E30 M3 MODELS

Paint – Standard saloons

There were four standard colours for the E30 M3 – Black, Red, Silver and White. However, the precise colours changed over time in line with changes elsewhere in the BMW colour palette. The variations are shown in the table below, together with production dates. The numbers are the BMW paint codes.

Black	Red	Silver	White
Diamond Black metallic – 181 (3/86 to 12/90)	Henna Red – 052 (3/86 to 8/87)	Salmon Silver metallic – 203 (3/86 to 8/89)	Alpine White – 146 (3/86 to 12/87)
	Cinnabar Red – 138 (9/87 to 8/89)	Sterling Silver metallic – 244 (9/89 to 12/90)	Alpine White II – 218 (1/88 to 12/90)
	Brilliant Red – 308 (9/89 to 12/90)		

Paint – Special saloons

Four colours were available only on special models, which in some cases also came in colours from the standard palette (see main text).

Black	Blue	Red	Silver
Jet Black – 668 (Sport Evolution)	Macao Blue metallic – 250 (Europameister, Evolution II, Cecotto and Ravaglia)	Misano Red – 236 (Europameister, Evolution II, Cecotto and Ravaglia)	Nogaro Silver metallic – 243 (Europameister, Evolution II, Cecotto and Ravaglia)

Paint – Convertibles

Convertibles were available in all the colours used on both standard and special saloons of the period. The full list of eight colours was:

Alpine White II – 218
Brilliant Red – 308
Diamond Black metallic – 181
Jet Black – 668

Macao Blue metallic – 250
Misano Red – 236
Nogaro Silver metallic – 243
Sterling Silver metallic – 244

Trim – Standard saloons

(a) Cloth

There were three basic colours for cloth trim: Beige, Grey and Silver.

Beige	Grey	Silver
Pearl Beige Country cloth – 0214 (3/86 to 8/87)	Anthracite Country cloth – 0211 (3/86 to 8/87)	Silver Uberkaro cloth – 0380 (9/87 to 12/90)
	Anthracite Uberkaro cloth – 0304/0379 (9/87 to 12/90)	
	Anthracite M-Technic cloth – 0461 (4/90 to 12/90)	

COLOURS AND TRIMS FOR E30 M3 MODELS *continued*

(b) Leather

There were four basic colours for leather trim: Beige, Black, Red and Silver.

Beige	*Black*	*Red*	*Silver*
Pearl Beige Bison leather – 0206 (3/86 to 8/87)	Black Bison leather – 0203 (3/86 to 12/90)	Cardinal Red Bison leather – 0256/0296 (3/86 to 8/89)	Silver Bison leather – 0292 (9/87 to 12/90)
Natur Bison leather –0295 (9/87 to 12/90)		Crimson Red Bison leather – 0324 (9/89 to 12/90)	

Trim – Special saloons

Model	Trim options
Europameister	Silver extended Nappa leather – 0319
Tour de Corse	Black Bison leather – 0203
Evolution II	Silver Uberkaro cloth w/ Silver Bison leather bolsters – 0305
Cecotto & Ravaglia	Anthracite M cloth with Black Bison leather bolsters – 0344 Silver M cloth with Silver Bison leather bolsters – 0345 Black Bison leather – 0203 Black extended Nappa leather – 0318 Silver extended Nappa leather – 0319
Sport Evolution	Anthracite M cloth – 0316 Black Nappa leather – 0393

Trim – Convertibles

There were seven trim options for the Convertibles. The leather option was always the 'extended' type, with Nappa leather. From March 1990, Convertibles could have Nappa Textil Webstruktur leather (code 785) in Black or Silver.

Cloth	*M-Sport cloth*	*Leather*
Anthracite – 0304	Anthracite – 0344	Black – 0226/0318
Silver – 0305	Silver – 0345	Lotus White – 0462
		Silver – 0227/0319

PERFORMANCE FIGURES FOR E30 M3 MODELS

Standard saloon	0–100km/h (0–62mph)	6.7 sec
	Maximum	235km/h (146mph)
Convertible	0–100km/h (0–62mph)	6.7 sec
	Maximum	232km/h (144mph)
Evolution II	0–100km/h (0–62mph)	6.7 sec
	Maximum	245km/h (152mph)
Sport Evolution III	0–100km/h (0–62mph)	6.5 sec
	Maximum	248km/h (154mph)

E30 M3 VIN CODES AND SEQUENCES

All E30 M3 models have a 17-digit Vehicle Identification Number (VIN). This consists of a ten-digit prefix and a seven-digit serial number. The serial number may consist of six numbers or a combination of letters and numbers.

A theoretical example would be:

WBSAK010XGA9876543

which decodes as shown below. Alternatives for each position are shown in the right-hand column.

WBS	BMW Motorsport GmbH, Munich
	WBA = BMW AG, Munich*
AK01	European-spec saloon without catalyst
	AK03 = North American-spec saloon with catalyst
	AK05 = European-spec saloon with catalyst
	AK07 = Sport Evolution
	BB01 = European-spec Convertible without catalyst
	BB05 = European-spec Convertible with catalyst
0	Manual safety belts
	1 = Belts and driver's airbag
X	Check digit (1–9, or X)
G	1986 model year
	H = 1987 L = 1990
	J = 1988 M = 1991
	K = 1989
9876543	Serial number
	(For more on these, see below.)

* The first 208 examples of the Sport Evolution carried the WBA prefix associated with non-Motorsport cars built by BMW. It is thought that the first 164 cars from 1986, all to European specification, also had the WBA prefix.

Serial numbers
The numbers quoted here are for first and last cars only. The BMW E30 cars shared common serial number ranges, and the M3 was a limited production model that was numbered in batches within those common ranges.

European non-catalyst models, October 1986 to July 1989
0842001–0845000
2190001–2192224
AE31000–AE31242

European catalyst models, October 1986 to May 1989
1891001–1894694
AE40000–AE40899

US catalyst models, December 1986 to December 1990
2195061–2198685
AE33000–AE34628

Evolution models, February to May 1987
2190005–2190787

Evolution II models, March to May 1988
Individual chassis numbers within main sequences

Europameister 88 Celebration models, October to November 1988
Individual chassis numbers within main sequences

Cecotto and Ravaglia models, April to July 1989
Individual chassis numbers within main sequences

215bhp models, September 1989 to December 1990
AE40900–AE42418

Sport Evolution III models, January to March 1990
AC79000–AC79599

Convertible models, first batch, March 1988 to October 1988
2001552
2385001–2385042
EB85001–EB85093

Convertible models, second batch, October 1988 to June 1989
2001613
3559001–3559088
EB86000–EB86085

Convertible models, third batch, March 1990 to June 1991
EB86086–EB86561

E30 M3 SPECIFICATIONS

Engines:

2.3-litre
Type S14B23 4-cylinder petrol
2302cc (93.4mm × 84mm)
Twin overhead camshafts, chain-driven
Four valves per cylinder
Five-bearing crankshaft
Compression ratio 10.5:1 for standard engines, 11.0:1 for Evolution II engines
Bosch Motronic ML fuel injection with DME control unit
200PS at 6,750rpm without catalytic converter (to July 1989 only)
195PS at 4,750rpm with catalytic converter (to July 1989 only)
239Nm (176lb ft) 4,750rpm without catalytic converter (to July 1989 only)
229Nm (169lb ft) at 4,750rpm with catalytic converter (to July 1989 only)
215PS at 6,750rpm with catalytic converter (from September 1989)
230Nm (170lb ft) at 4,600rpm
220PS at 6750rpm with catalytic converter (Evolution II only)
245Nm (181lb ft) at 4,750rpm

2.5-litre
(Sport Evolution III only)
Type S14B25 4-cylinder petrol
2467cc (95mm × 87mm)
Twin overhead camshafts, chain-driven
Four valves per cylinder
Five-bearing crankshaft
Compression ratio 10.2:1
Bosch Motronic ML fuel injection with DME control unit
238PS at 7000rpm
240Nm (177lb ft) at 4,750rpm
Catalytic converter standard

Transmission:
Five-speed Getrag 265 manual gearbox standard
Ratios 3.72:1, 2.40:1, 1.77:1, 1.26:1, 1.00:1; reverse 3.25:1
Five-speed Getrag 'Sport' manual gearbox for North American and Japanese models
Ratios 3.83:1, 2.20:1, 1.40:1, 1.00:1, 0.81:1; reverse 3.91:1

Axle ratio:
Standard 3.25:1
3.15:1 on Evolution II and Sport Evolution III models
4.10:1 on North American and Japanese models

Suspension, steering and brakes:
Front suspension with MacPherson struts, coil springs, Boge gas dampers and anti-roll bar
Rear suspension with semi-trailing arms, Minibloc coil springs, Boge gas dampers and anti-roll bar
Rack-and-pinion steering with 19.6:1 ratio and standard power assistance
Disc brakes all round, 280mm (11in) ventilated on front wheels and 282mm (11.1in) solid on rear wheels; twin hydraulic circuits; ABS standard

Dimensions:

Overall length:	4,360mm (171.6in)
Overall width:	1,675mm (65.9in)
Overall height:	1,370mm (53.9in) for saloons
	1,360mm (53.5in) for Convertibles
Wheelbase:	2,562mm (100.9in)
Front track:	1,412mm (55.6in)
Rear track:	1,424mm (56.1in)

Wheels and tyres:
7J × 15 five-stud alloy wheels with 205/55 ZR 15 tyres
7.5J × 16 five-stud alloy wheels with 225/45ZR16 tyres on Evolution II and Sport Evolution III models

Unladen weights:

Standard saloon	1,285kg/2,833lb
Convertible	1,415kg/3,120lb

PRODUCTION FIGURES FOR E30 M3 MODELS

	Saloon	Convertible	Overall
1986	2,397		2,397
1987	6,396		6,396
1988	3,426	130	3,556
1989	2,541	180	2,721
1990	2,424	176	2,600
1991		300	300
Total	17,184	786	**17,970**

The figures for individual types of saloon are shown below.

European non-cat (200PS)	3/86 to 8/89	5,187	Includes Evolution and Evolution II
European with cat (195PS)	5/86 to 5/89	4,585	Includes Europameister edition, plus six special-order cars built in 1/90
European 215PS	9/89 to 12/90	1,512	Includes Cecotto & Ravaglia editions and Swiss Cecotto edition
Sport Evolution 238PS	12/89 to 3/90	600	
North American	3/87 to 12/90	5,300	USA: 5115 Canada: 185
		17,184	

The figures for the special edition saloons are shown separately below.

	Dates	Total
Evolution (includes French Tour de Corse edition)	2/87 to 5/87	505
Evolution II	3/88 to 6/88	501
Sport Evolution	12/89 to 3/90	600
Europameister 88	10/88 to 11/88	148
Cecotto	4/89 to 7/89	480
Ravaglia	6/89	25
Overall total		**2,259**

UK 'official' imports were as shown below. They include imports of the limited editions (7 of the original M3 Evolution, 51 of the Evolution II and 45 of the Sport Evolution III). Some UK cars have subsequently gone abroad, and other non-UK models have been brought into the country.

	Saloon	Convertible	Overall
1987	55		55
1988	58		58
1989	62	19	81
1990	36	13	49
1991	25	1	26
1992	21		21
Total	257	33	**290**

CHAPTER THREE

DRIVING, BUYING, SPECIAL EDITIONS AND THE COMPETITION M3

If the E30 M3 had started out as a homologation special that allowed BMW to go racing, it was certainly not long before the company's marketing men realized that an essential element in its customer appeal was exclusivity. So they soon began to trade on this fact, and between 1987 and 1990 BMW sold a number of special-edition models that offered a little extra exclusivity – at extra cost, of course.

This practice rapidly became an important part of the M3 story. As the later chapters in this book show, limited-edition and special-edition M3s soon became familiar fare – perhaps too familiar by the time the fourth-generation E90-series cars were approaching the end of their production run, as Chapter 10 suggests.

During the E30's production life, however, the special editions did seem to have an additional purpose. Every one of them was linked in some way to successes in motor sport, for which the M3 had been designed in the first place.

THE TOUR DE CORSE EDITION (1987)

BMW France created their own special edition in 1987 to celebrate a win by the French team of Bernard Beguin and Jean-Jacques Lenne in that year's Tour de Corse rally. This was a tarmac event held on twisty mountain roads in Corsica and was then part of the World Rally Championship. Beguin's M3, with rally number 10, held off two Lancia HF Integrale rally cars to win the event; a second M3 finished in sixth place.

There were fifty examples of the Tour de Corse edition, each one with a numbered plaque on the dashboard that carried the facsimile signatures of Beguin and Lenne. The

cars were probably all built in April 1987, and were based on the first-series Evolution model.

The cars were all painted in Diamond Black and BMW France fitted them with 7.5 × 16 cross-spoke alloy wheels. The M3 grille badge was replaced by a Tour de Corse badge and there was a Tour de Corse decal on the left-hand side of the boot lid. The cars had 1986-specification yellow headlamps to suit French regulations of the time.

There was Black leather upholstery, and all four seats had Motorsport tricolour labels. The kick plates had M3 logos and there was an M footrest. Other standard equipment included central locking, an electric sunroof, electric windows, a headlamp wash-wipe, velour floor mats, an interior headlamp adjuster, a dash-mounted ICE fader control and an on-board computer.

THE EUROPAMEISTER 88 CELEBRATION EDITION (1988)

The 1988 season was very successful for the BMW M3 Group A cars, which dominated the tracks throughout and achieved an overall win in the hands of driver Roberto Ravaglia. So BMW lost no time in creating a special edition of the M3 – the first of its kind – to capitalize on this success.

The special edition consisted of 1989-model cars built between October and December 1988, and went under the name of Europameister 88 Celebration (Europameister translates as 'European Champion'). All were painted in Macao Blue metallic (code 250) and there were 150 examples, or 148 according to some sources. At heart, they were standard M3 models, with the 195PS catalyst-equipped engine. However, they did have the Evolution-type extended front spoiler and twin-blade rear spoiler, and there were

16-inch BBS wheels with 7.5-inch rims, black-enamelled spokes and 225/45ZR16 Pirelli P700 tyres.

The majority had 'extended' leather upholstery in Silver Nappa leather – 'extended' meant that the leather was also used on the centre console and on the special diagonally pleated door panels. All four seats also had M-stripe labels. At extra cost, the leather trim could be extended even further, to cover the whole dashboard, the glovebox lid and the steering wheel rim, but this option was expensive enough to remain rare.

All the Europameister cars had M3-branded door kick plates and an M footrest for the driver. Their centre consoles carried a plate reading 'Europameister 1988 auf BMW M3' ('European Champion in a BMW M3') with the signature of driver Roberto Ravaglia, plus the car's number within the special edition. Otherwise, only a green-tinted windscreen strip and electric windows were out of the ordinary. It does appear, though, that many examples were equipped with multiple options.

None of these cars came to the UK through official BMW channels although individuals may have imported examples in more recent years.

THE JOHNNY CECOTTO EDITION (1989)

No doubt encouraged by customer response to the Europameister special edition, BMW decided to use a second special edition to preview the new 215PS engine that would not become standard for other European-specification M3s until the arrival of the 1990 models in September 1989.

This second special edition was introduced in April 1989, and for most markets was known as the Johnny Cecotto edition. However, endless confusion has resulted from two things: first, that the cars for the UK market were numbered within the Cecotto series but were known by another name; and second, that there was a special and completely separate Cecotto edition for Switzerland for the 1990 model year that was not numbered at all.

Johnny Cecotto was a successful M3 driver, who piloted a car on behalf of BMW that had been prepared by Schnitzer Motorsport (better known outside Germany as tuning specialist AC Schnitzer). The M3 edition that bore his name had a number of visual similarities to the Evolution II, coming in the same three colours of Macao Blue metallic, Misano Red and Nogaro Silver metallic. It had the same front and rear

With the Cecotto edition of 480 cars, BMW not only celebrated the triumphs of a successful driver but also explored further the market for special editions of the M3.

The Cecotto edition cars had half-leather seats with striped Motorsport cloth wearing surfaces. Though not clear in this picture, the gearshift knob was also illuminated – just the sort of detail that M3 enthusiasts would come to expect.

Another experiment: would M3 buyers take to red paint on the cam cover and plenum chamber? BMW tried it out on the Cecotto cars.

spoilers as the Evolution II, but had fog lights in the front apron rather than brake-cooling ducts. The cars had 16-inch wheels with 7.5-inch rims, metallic-black enamelled spokes and Pirelli P700Z 225/45ZR 16 tyres; chromed exhaust tail-pipes; a green windscreen top strip; and, less obviously, the thinner glass of the Evolution II models.

Under the bonnet, the engine had been further developed, came as standard with an exhaust catalyst (because cars without one could not be sold in West Germany from 1989) and developed 215PS. Torque remained at the same 230Nm (170lb ft) as before, but now at the lower engine speed of 4,600rpm. Again, BMW had attended to cosmetic detail under the bonnet: the engines of the Cecotto edition cars had their cam covers and plenum chambers painted in red.

The cabin had seats trimmed in half-leather, with Anthracite or Silver M-Technic striped cloth combined with Bison leather bolsters. Buyers were not limited to this however, and could order Black Bison leather, Black extended Nappa leather or Silver extended Nappa leather if they were prepared to pay extra for the privilege. Standard equipment included electric windows, a headlight height-adjustment control, an on-board computer and a cassette tape storage box. Also standard on the Cecotto cars were M3-branded sill kick plates, an M footrest for the driver, an illuminated

gearshift grip and, of course, a numbered plaque on the centre console carrying the signature of Johnny Cecotto.

As far as BMW were concerned, there were 505 of these cars, and they were numbered on those console plaques accordingly. However, twenty-five cars were built for the UK as the Roberto Ravaglia edition (see below), with the result that there were actually only 480 Cecotto cars.

THE ROBERTO RAVAGLIA EDITION (1989)

Exactly why the UK importers chose not to take the Cecotto edition in standard form is not clear, but the most probable explanation is that Cecotto was far less well known in the UK than on the European continent. AC Schnitzer, for whom Cecotto's success were achieved, were also not widely recognized in the UK at the time. So, as the UK had not taken any of the Europameister 88 Celebration editions 'signed' by Ravaglia, BMW UK chose to have his signature in the April 1989 special-edition cars.

There were just twenty-five Ravaglia cars in this edition, sixteen of them in Misano Red with Anthracite half-leather upholstery and the remaining nine in Nogaro Silver metallic with Silver half-leather upholstery. They all had a numbered plaque on the centre console with Ravaglia's signature rather than Cecotto's but in all other respects were the same as the Cecotto cars.

THE SWISS M3 CECOTTO EDITION (1989)

Switzerland had its own, particularly strict, emissions control regulations in place by the end of the 1990s, and so BMW Switzerland had to handle M3 sales their own way. During the 1990 model year (and therefore somewhat later than in other countries) they had their own M3 Cecotto special edition of eighty cars.

The cars were identical in almost every respect to the 1989-model Cecotto models for other markets, but they had three important differences: first, they had a special 211PS version of the 2.3-litre engine, tuned to suit Swiss emissions regulations; second, they had the M-Technic II steering wheel associated with all 1990-model M3s; and third, the console-mounted plaque bearing the signature of Johnny Cecotto did not carry a limited-edition number.

These eighty Swiss cars were built in two batches, the first in October and November 1989 and the second in April and May 1990.

THE E30 M3 IN COMPETITION, 1987–1991

From the very beginning, the E30 M3 was designed as a competition car, and the road car was then developed from that design as a somewhat softer and more practical derivative. Although the E30 M3 was thus much closer in spirit to a competition car than any later car to wear the

M3 badge, it was certainly not the same car that a number of teams with BMW backing fielded on the tracks between 1987 and 1991.

The basic work on the car had been done a long time before BMW Motorsport got together with a number of specialist suppliers to develop the Group A Touring Car specification for the 1987 season. That work, which was in effect fine-tuning of the basic design, took place between the summer of 1986 and the first months of 1987, and led to an initial competition specification.

BMW then built a total of 330 competition M3s, 270 for Group A events and 60 for Group N events, according to BMW racing team manager Karsten Engel. These were addi-

This picture gives some idea of the differences between the road-going M3 and the track cars of 1987. Note the absence of a sunroof, single windscreen wiper, the smaller (and more aerodynamic) mirrors and the huge strut brace behind the engine on the racing derivative. Quite obvious, too, is that the racer has only one seat inside.

tional to the road cars and have their own complex and fascinating history. They were supplied as 'kits', to be built up and prepared by the various racing and rallying organizations that campaigned them. They also had their own numbering system with a three-digit prefix (always 'M3 1') and a one-, two- or three-digit serial number (e.g. 9, 37 or 101) to give a complete number such as M3 1 101. Build dates can generally be established by a plate on the roll cage that was installed by Matter during preparation of the body shells.

Many of these cars were sold on to other teams after their international careers were over. Some were damaged in accidents and either written off or re-shelled. There is considerable interest in establishing the histories of all the competition E30 M3s, and for anyone interested a good place to start is www.ten-tenths.com/forum. Research regularly turns up new information, and it would be pointless even to summarize what is known here, as it would quickly become out of date.

One additional result of the E30 M3's competition history is that a number of the road cars have been turned into very effective club or historic racers. Nevertheless, these are not at all comparable to the genuine competition machines of the 1987–91 period.

THE RACING RESULTS

E30 M3s were raced by a number of major teams with BMW factory support during the 1987–91 seasons. Schnitzer were usually the front runners, but there were strong perform-

ances from Team Linder, Zakspeed (to 1990), Cibiemme and Team Bigazzi; also important were Prodrive in the UK.

The M3's competition success was not limited to the international scene. At lower levels of competition, small teams competed in national events in the car of the moment, hoping to move up to greater things. BMW Motorsport were always prepared to provide competition kits to keen amateur drivers who had the funds. Engine tuning was, however, down to the customer, who had to find his or her own specialist.

1987

The M3's first season in international competition saw it achieve a magnificent result: overall winner of the first (and

Driver Roberto Ravaglia is seen here piloting the M3 at the Jarama circuit near Madrid during 1987.

An M3 on a rally stage: this was Bernard Beguin in a Group A car, on his way to victory in the 1987 Tour de Corse.

only) World Touring Car Championship series in the hands of the Schnitzer team, with Roberto Ravaglia at the wheel. Ravaglia achieved no fewer than four outright wins in tandem with co-driver Emanuele Pirro.

There was also a spectacular win for an M3 in the Tour de Corse, which was an event in the first ever World Rally Championship (a series not continued for 1988 because of huge controversies). Drivers Bernard Beguin and Jean-Jacques Lenne drove a Prodrive-prepared car

to victory. Winfried 'Winni' Vogt secured the Group A European Touring Car Championship in an M3 prepared by Team Linder and Eric van de Poele claimed the German Touring Car Championship in a Zakspeed-prepared car. Five more national titles fell to M3s in 1987 – those of Australia, Finland, France, Holland and Portugal. In addition, and in a separate sphere of motor sport, the M3 took the Group A Trophy for makes in the European Hill-climb Championship.

TOP: **Its racing career now over, one of the Zakspeed DTM cars is seen at a display.** WIKIMEDIA/STAHLKOCHER

1988

The Schnitzer team were again to the fore in the 1988 season, when Ravaglia took the drivers' title in the European Touring Car Championship series. Right behind them in second place was a Prodrive-prepared car, and Prodrive prepared the winning cars in both the British and Belgian national championships, the former being driven by Frank Sytner and the latter by Patrick Snijers with Dany Colebunders. M3s also claimed national titles in the Asia-Pacific, Dutch, French, Portuguese and Swedish championships.

1989

There was no European Touring Car Championship for 1989, but the M3 continued to shine in national championships. Particularly important to BMW among these was a win at home against Mercedes-Benz in the German championships. Prodrive-prepared cars also won the Belgian and French titles, and M3s claimed rally championship titles in the Netherlands, Spain and Yugoslavia.

MIDDLE AND LEFT: **Eric van de Poele, seen here with his racing M3, drove for the Zakspeed team. The same car is also seen in action on the track.**

This was one of the Team Linder cars.

1990

National titles that fell to the M3 in 1990 were those of Belgium, Finland, Italy, the Netherlands and Switzerland. In the British championships, an M3 came second; in the German championship, Johnny Cecotto took a Schnitzer-prepared car to second place while Team Bigazzi's Steve Soper came fourth.

Particularly notable was a 1-2-3 finish by the M3s at the 24 Hours of Spa race, the drivers being Johnny Cecotto, Fabien Giroix and Markus Oesterreich.

1991

BMW were a team down for 1991, as Zakspeed defected to Mercedes-Benz. As in 1990, the German national title went to Audi, but the M3s achieved some excellent results in sprint and long-distance races.

THE COMPETITION E30 M3

The first Group A racing E30 M3s appeared in 1987. In subsequent years, the M3 was developed further to remain competitive and to keep up with changing regulations. There were also cars prepared for Group N events, and a number were prepared for rallying events, notably by Prodrive in the UK.

Bodyshell

Key to the racing M3's bodyshell was considerable reinforcement in strategic areas, using lightweight steel, while a rollover cage (made by Matter) was mounted inside the passenger cabin. The overall result was said in 1987 to be a massive 300 per cent improvement in torsional rigidity over the standard car.

The interior trim was, of course, stripped out and

replaced by the bare essentials needed for racing. There was also a larger fuel tank, capable of carrying 110 litres (24.2 gallons) of fuel. The fuel was actually carried in a 'bag tank' suspended within a Kevlar outer structure for safety.

Despite the additional weight of these components, the typical overall weight of a Group A M3 in 1987 was 960kg (2,116lb) – considerably lighter than the 1,200kg (2,646lb) of a standard production car.

Wheels, tyres and brakes

The racing M3s used centre-lock wheels to permit rapid wheel changes. The favoured types were made by BBS and were three-piece alloys with magnesium centres and a 9J×17 size. These ran on 245/610×17 tyres; Pirellis were favoured at the start of the season but many teams switched to Yokohama tyres in mid-season. Some teams preferred 16-inch wheels with 235/590×16 tyres, and yet others combined 16-inch front wheels with 17-inch rears in order to give sharper steering.

Typical brakes in the 1987 season had 332mm (13.1in) ventilated front discs (32mm thick) with four-piston calipers by Brembo. The rear brakes were also ventilated, though with the standard 280mm (11in) diameter and a 20.7mm width, and also had four-piston calipers. There was no ABS at this stage.

Suspension and steering

The whole suspension was lowered by 40mm (1.6in) as compared to the road cars, and minor dimensional changes meant that the wheelbase of the racers was 2,565.5mm (101.00in) rather than the standard 2,562mm (100.87in).

The front suspension had Bilstein aluminium tube struts with low-pressure gas dampers and much stiffer spring rates. There were cross-braced lower front suspension arms made from forged aluminium, and cast magnesium uprights. The suspension was rose-jointed and the anti-roll bar was adjustable, while adjustable spring plates enabled the ride height to be varied to suit individual tracks.

The rear suspension had reinforced semi-trailing arms with pivot-bearing mounting points. Camber and castor were quickly adjustable, to suit individual tracks, and once again the anti-roll bar could be adjusted as well.

All the hubs were special, to suit the centre-lock wheels, and the steering dispensed with the power assistance of the road cars and had a quicker rack with a 17:1 ratio.

Engine and drivetrain

The Group A regulations allowed a slight increase in capacity, and so the engines of the 1987 cars were given a 94mm bore, which resulted in a swept volume of 2332cc (more precisely, 2331.8cc). New pistons took the compression ratio up to 12:1.

Exact engine outputs are impossible to quote, not least because they varied from one car to the next, and from one event to the next as well. The BMW Press Department claimed at the time that power was increased by 50 per cent over the standard 200PS of the non-cat cars, which would give 300PS. That figure was probably a little optimistic, and somewhere nearer 285–290PS was perhaps more accurate, developed at 8,000rpm. Maximum torque was increased, to 270Nm (199lb ft), but it arrived at a very high 7,000rpm.

The Getrag five-speed, close-ratio gearbox remained the racers' choice, but a variety of final drives was available and a choice was made at each event to suit the track. Options ranged from 3.15:1 to 5.28:1. A factory demonstration using a 4.41:1 final drive delivered acceleration of 0–100km/h (0–62mph) in 4.6 seconds, and BMW claimed speeds as high as 280km/h (174mph) on a 3.25:1 final drive.

The later cars

As development proceeded to make the cars more and more competitive, specifications changed. For the 1988 season, the new front and rear spoilers showcased on the Evolution road cars became standard wear. Some teams began using 9J×18 wheels and six-speed gearboxes, by either Getrag or Prodrive. Lightweight panels became available (and had in fact been available in 1987 but had been declared illegal and had earned the M3s a ban at Monza).

For 1989, the primary focus was on obtaining higher engine revolutions and more power. At the start of the season, 8,800rpm was considered the safe rev limit, but this rose gradually, to 9,200rpm over the summer and to 9,800rpm by the end of the season. The official figures for the racing cars were nevertheless 320PS at 8,500rpm with 272 Nm (201lb ft) of torque at 7,000rpm. BMW claimed a 300km/h

(186mph) maximum speed, depending of course on the final drive chosen. The cars raced at the minimum permitted weight of 1,040kg (2,292lb), although the Motorsport engineers claimed that 940kg (2,072lb) would have been possible.

Engine changes for the 1989 cars included a stronger crankcase, lighter pistons, lighter camshafts, double injectors and BMW's own ECU in place of the Motronic type. In the German Touring Car Championship, regulations differed from those in the international Group A events, and the cars were able to run with slide throttle air intakes, which gave a little extra power.

The engine size increased for the 1990 season, as reflected in that year's Evolution II road cars. Development of the racing versions started in July 1989, and by the time they reached the tracks the engines had a slightly larger bore of 95.5mm, which gave 2467cc with the standard stroke. On a 12:1 compression ratio, power was claimed to be 330PS at 8,500rpm, while torque peaked at 7,500rpm with around 290Nm (214lb ft). These were lower-revving engines than seen in the 1988 season, beginning the season with a safe rev limit of 9,200rpm and ending it with a 9,500rpm limit. As an indication of the progress made since the beginning, the 1990 cars could lap the Nürburgring in a huge eight seconds less than the 1987 racers. During 1990, some teams also switched to new brake calipers made by AP Racing.

The main news for the 1991 season was the development of an ABS system that was suitable for track use. Tested over the winter of 1990/91, it had been developed by BMW Motorsport in conjunction with braking specialists Alfred Teves GmbH, and could be switched off from the dashboard if the driver so wished. It was not fitted to every factory-supported M3 in the 1991 season, however. Brake disc sizes also increased in this final year, typically to 350mm (13.8in) at the front and 300mm (11.8in) at the rear, as often as not with six-piston calipers.

However, 1991 was the last season for full factory sponsorship of the E30 M3 in racing events. Although the car continued to be campaigned by privateers for several more years, BMW Motorsport moved on to other things when the E30 went out of production.

Not every racing M3 used the new 2.5-litre engine in 1990 and beyond. Some continued to run with 2.3-litre engines, and to meet regulations in the British championships the engines actually had a swept volume of just 2.0 litres.

To meet regulations obtaining in British touring car events, Prodrive developed a 2.0-litre engine for the M3, with a 1989cc swept volume from a standard 93.4mm bore

allied to a short-stroke crankshaft giving 72.6mm of piston movement. These engines typically put out 265bhp.

Prodrive also came up with a six-speed, non-synchromesh gearbox, designed for them by John Piper and manufactured by racing transmission specialists Xtrac. The gear ratios were 2.449:1, 1.913:1, 1.579:1, 1.332:1, 1.148:1 and 1.000:1.

The Prodrive rally cars

The Prodrive rally cars were primarily designed for tarmac rallies, but were not really competitive in the gravel events of the World Rally Championship, where four-wheel drive and turbocharged engines gradually became dominant and the Lancia Delta Integrale was the car of the moment.

Nevertheless, the Prodrive rally car won its very first event (the 1987 Tour de Corse), and over the next four years or so won a number of titles in Belgian, French and Irish events. The primary drivers were Marc Duez (Belgium), Bernard Beguin and Francois Chatriot (France) and Bertie Fisher and Austin McHale (Ireland).

SO YOU WANT TO BUY AN E30 M3?

By the time this book was being written in 2013, the E30 M3 had passed beyond its fast everyday road-car period and had become a firm fixture in the classic car pantheon. That change has been a double-edged sword in a way. It means that really good examples are likely to be bought by people who know what they are and will look after them, but it also means that rough examples that come up for sale will be accompanied by unrealistic price tags. Rough examples – and that includes cars that have been used hard as club racers – are best avoided because they will not only fail to live up to the E30 M3's formidable reputation but will also cost a small fortune in repairs and maintenance.

A really good E30 M3, by contrast, will be a delightful car to own. UK buyers might regret its LHD-only configuration, but this need not be seen as a major handicap. The cars were very well built, essentially reliable, and are instantly-recognizable head-turners. Few buyers can ask for more in a classic car.

When inspecting a potential purchase, a good check of the bodywork and general structure will reveal a lot about the car's history. Many cars – even those that have been well

In 1987, BMW provided an M3 as a 'Ring Taxi' for use at the Nürburgring. Here is Motorsport director Wolfgang Peter Flohr at the wheel on the occasion of the handover ceremony.

Australian artist Ken Done created this Art Car in 1989 from a Group A racing M3. The car was new in 1987 and was used by the Motorsport division of BMW Australia, being run by the JPS-BMW Team. Jim Richards drove it to victory in the Australian Group A Driver's Championship, but the car raced only once during 1988 and was then withdrawn from competition events and earmarked as the 'canvas' for Ken Done.

THE E30 M3 IN ITS OWN TIME

A quarter of a century on from the days when the E30 M3 was a current model, perceptions of the car have become coloured by legend and by subsequent events. However, it is possible to get a clear picture of how the cars were perceived when they were new by looking at contemporary press reports.

What Car? October 1986
Particularly impressive at [...] high speeds was the car's stability: BMW's time spent developing the cars' aerodynamics and suspension has not been wasted. If the car does have a fault, then it becomes apparent during motorway cruising. Fifth gear is a direct top and not an overdrive, and as a consequence the engine always feels slightly strained and uncomfortable while cruising.

Take the car off motorways and onto open, twisting roads and the M3 comes alive. It is extremely well balanced in all aspects. The engine pulls strongly from well down, gaining strength beyond the 4,000rpm mark and continuing right round to the red-line in each gear until maximum in fifth is reached.

The handling is a delight, precise and vice-free. Admittedly, the rear wheels can be made to slide out of line, but the LSD prevents any sudden breakaway and a touch of opposite lock will soon balance the car and have it pointing the right way.

[…] The driving position is near ideal, with the pedals perfectly located for heel-and-toeing. The car being left-hand drive, its gear change can catch the British out at times – especially from fourth to third – but practice makes perfect.

Autocar, 3 June 1987
The M3 is free [...] from circuit-induced compromises; the ride is taut but only feels stiff around town, while the interior is that of the 3-Series at its most luxurious, including sports front buckets and leather seat trim.

The M3's most impressive aspect, though, is the transformation to handling and roadholding. What looks on paper to be tuning rather than changing the suspension has produced a 3-Series that steers tautly,

rolls little, and above all handles neutrally. Uprated brakes have also made a substantial improvement to stopping. This car is a treat, and a revelation, to drive.

AutoSport, 9 July 1987
If, perchance, you hook second gear by mistake, the engine has quite sufficient torque not to leave you floundering at traffic lights.

[...] The rewards of driving the car quickly and smoothly are exceptionally high, for its inherent balance, tremendous mid-range flexibility, lightning quick response to turn-in commands and solid, reassuring, feel inspire confidence beyond the realms of normal everyday motoring. The M3 is a competition car, and does not let you forget it.

Car & Driver, November 1987
Let's put an end to the BMW-yuppie links. [...] That over-publicized group of consumers, who lust after Bimmers as they do any object perceived to confer status on its owners, could never fully appreciate the car you see on these pages.

[...] Best of all, the M3's power delivery is wonderfully linear; it pulls willingly from its midrange all the way to its sizzling 7,250-rpm redline.

[At the Lime Rock track in Connecticut] The M3 leaps through the corners like a cat, its feisty engine spinning and spitting until you snatch another gear or the rev limiter grabs it by the tail.

Automobile, December 1987
We may have felt more obvious on the street than we usually prefer...

Autosport, 3 August 1989
The Convertible is every bit as brilliant in the corners as the standard M3. [...] As an utterly exhilarating cross-country machine, on a bright sunny day, the M3 Convertible is near perfection. [...] Top up, you have to be cruising at the ton or more before wind thrash on the roof drowns out normal conversation.

looked after – may have been involved in accidents, and it is advisable to check very carefully for evidence of this. Poor panel fit, uneven panel gaps and wavy or rippled panels are just the first indication.

One giveaway is the seam where the top corner of each front wing meets the windscreen surround. There should be a line of seam-sealer, sprayed over in the body colour. If not, the front wings have been off the car, and the only good reason for taking them off is to replace them after a front-end collision. If they have been replaced, did the body shop use original steel items, pattern steel items, or GRP pattern parts? That line of seam-sealer is not a guarantee that the wings have never been off, of course – but only a very careful restorer will have bothered to replace it to make it look the way it did when the car left the BMW factory.

As all E30 M3s are at least 22 years old, a little rust in the structure or on the panels is only to be expected. Panel rust will be obvious, but it is important to look in the less obvious places as well. Rust may have begun to attack the door bottoms (underneath, not just in the visible outer panel) and the structural body sills that are hidden behind the plastic side-skirts. Other important places to check are the longitudinal members that strengthen the floorpan, and in the front footwells.

The general appearance of the engine can also reveal something about the car's history. Oil leaks and untidy wiring are always a bad sign, but a suspiciously clean engine may have been steam-cleaned prior to sale to help hide such leaks. The common sources of oil leaks are the head and sump gaskets, the oil-pressure relief valve on the oil-filter housing, and the crankshaft seal on the timing cover at the front of the engine. Dirty or low oil is another bad sign; regular oil changes are essential to keep the engine in good health, and some experts even recommend that only modern synthetic oil is used.

It is best to start the engine from completely cold in order to show up any faults. The oil light should go out immediately, and a delay here could well indicate that there is a problem with the oil pump or that the crankshaft bearings are on the way out. A healthy engine will idle smoothly and without a lot of noise from the valvetrain – although some noise from this area is only to be expected. The timing chain should not be noisy either, and it is important to check when it was last changed. In normal use, it lasts only 60–70,000 miles without stretching.

Odd or irregular noises need further investigation, perhaps even including a compression check of each cylinder. A lumpy tickover points to trouble, and one common cause is that the flexible mountings between inlet manifold and cylinder head can perish, so disturbing the fuel/air mixture. A smell of burning oil under the bonnet may indicate a leaking valve cover gasket, and a particular failing of the M3's engine is that the oil seals on the spark plug holes can deteriorate and fail to exclude stray oil, which then leads to misfiring. An odd one to look out for is worn alternator bushes, and odd alternator noises or a drive belt that seems to run at an angle (when viewed from the right-hand side of the car) will be good indicators of this.

It is best to check for gearbox problems during a test drive. Most problems will be obvious – jumping out of gear, worn synchromesh and so on – but the gearbox mountings can also deteriorate, and this leads to a vague feel in the gear lever, hard or notchy gear selection (especially when the gearbox moves on its mountings in cornering) and often to a lot of movement in the lever under hard acceleration or braking.

Underneath the car, check for oil leaks, which commonly occur from both the gearbox and the final drive. There should be no play in the propshaft universal joints, nor should there be any splits in the shaft's flexible coupling. Any twists or ripples in the transverse beam that carries the final drive probably indicate accident damage, so investigate further. This beam is attached to the body at each end by a large bush, and these can deteriorate, so allowing the rear 'axle' to move relative to the body and deliver unpredictable handling. The final drive itself is carried on a large rubber mounting, and this will cause an assortment of clunks and bangs at the rear if it is worn.

Split rubber boots around the ball joints on the front suspension can let road dirt in and allow grease to seep out. Play in any of the top or bottom joints will lead to such things as steering shimmy, knocking noises from the front end and imprecise handling. Failed bushes on the lower front wishbones will cause vague steering or vibration at motorway speeds. For road use, there is little point in replacing these bushes with uprated types, but it is important to remember that the M3 bushes are harder than their standard E30 equivalents.

One final word of advice is to call in an independent BMW specialist for a second opinion on the serviceability of any E30 M3 considered as a purchase. The small cost of such an opinion is far preferable to the sinking feeling that accompanies the realization that a car was not the good purchase it seemed to be after all.

CHAPTER FOUR

REFINEMENT REPLACES RAW POWER – THE E36 M3, 1992–99

BMW started work on its second-generation 3 Series range in the first half of the 1980s, and fundamental to the product brief was that the new models should have a wider appeal than the existing E30 models. So the range of body options was to be wider: central to the new range would be a four-door saloon and a four-door estate, and the two-door style (now rechristened a coupé) and related convertible would become the icing on the cake. There would also be a two-door Compact model, shortened at the rear end to compete in the hatchback market. It was all very different from the E30 range, where two-door models had been the only ones available. To accommodate the four-door bodies and give more interior room, the new E36 models were made bigger, and they were given a much more modern appeal with a new, sleek and more rounded appearance.

The standard E36 3 Series was an elegantly proportioned car although the blacked-out sills just visible in this shot of a saloon model tended to make it look heavier than it was.

This early M3 Coupé shows the subtle makeover that delivered the Motorsport version of the E36. Clear are the special front apron, multi-spoke wheels, door mirrors and sill panels. The Dakar Yellow paint was also unique to the M3. Note that there was no model identification on the grille – but there was an M3 badge on the front door bump-strip.

As design progressed, the likely requirements of the Motorsport division were of course taken into account, but it must have been clear right from the start that the M3 derivatives of the E36 range would be based on the two-door cars – the Coupé and Convertible. In due course, there were also M3 saloons – which stood in for the absence of an M5 four-door saloon between 1994 and 1997 – but there would never be an M3 version of the estate, which BMW called the Touring.

It was the four-door saloon that introduced the E36 range to the world at the Frankfurt Motor Show in autumn 1990, and the other three body variants followed one by one. First to arrive was the Coupé, in January 1992, and that opened the door for the new E36 M3 to be announced as well. The Convertible appeared in 1993, and that was of course followed by an M3 Convertible; the Compact made its bow in 1994; and then the Touring estate followed in 1995.

Not only did the order of events arranged for the E36 body types have its impact on the shape of the new M3

range but so did the whole nature of the E36 range. The E30s had been exclusively 4-cylinder cars, but the E36 range was scheduled to feature a number of small-capacity 6-cylinder engines. So it was quite obvious from early on that the new M3 would have to have a 6-cylinder engine, and that would make the car very different in character from the original M3.

The more upmarket pretensions of the new E36 range also meant that the new M3s would have a different character. In a nutshell, the E36 M3 would replace the raw excitement of its E30 predecessor with refinement. It would all tie in perfectly with the M3's growing importance as an automotive status symbol rather than as an exotic homologation special, and the second-generation models would go on to become as much about high specification as high performance. They would be built in larger numbers, too. The E36 M3 would be put together on the main M3 assembly lines at BMW's Regensburg factory, and would not be hand-finished at the BMW M GmbH plant in Garching.

Development testing: the special hardware of the M3 models was developed in cars that were outwardly identical to the standard E36 Coupé, like this one. Note the different front and rear wheels.

THE M3 COUPÉ, 1992

So the first of the E36 M3s was a Coupé, introduced in 1992. Its basic bodyshell was of course shared with the other new E36 Coupés, but there was no mistaking it for any of the lesser-engined cars. Immediately obvious was the M Sport styling, which consisted of special spoilers and sills but was far too well integrated into the car's overall appearance to be described as a 'body kit'.

The standard E36 of the time had a rather unflattering collection of dark plastic bumper valances and sills, but the M3 dispensed with these altogether. Instead, it had a deep front apron spoiler in the body colour, containing a similarly painted central mesh grille that was flanked by a pair of fog lights. Also in body colour were special sills with a fluted crossover pattern that disguised their real depth, and there was a deeper rear valance than standard, once again in body colour and also featuring aerodynamic extensions.

59

The door mirrors with their twin stalks were undeniably stylish.

The door mirrors, too, were special, with a bullet-like shape mounted on a pair of aerodynamic 'legs'. It would be BMW Motorsport policy to brand most of its products with special names during the 1990s, and these mirrors were no exception: they were called M Style aerodynamic mirrors.

Oddly perhaps, there was no M3 identification on the radiator grille. Instead, the M3 logo was embedded in the bump strips towards the front edge of each door, and there was then a discreet M3 logo on the right-hand side of the

ABOVE: **Identification may not have been on the grille, but it was unmissable on the wheels, which had the Motorsport name cast into their centres.**

LEFT: **Sills, bump-strips and door mirrors were all unique to the M3 models.**

boot lid. The alloy wheels were a special ten-spoke design with 'BMW Motorsport' branding around their centre sections, and had a 17-inch diameter to give maximum room for the enlarged brake discs.

Immediately apparent on opening a door were the special M Sport seats, upholstered as standard in cloth but with Amaretta suede bolsters. The front pair had an adjustable upper third and their head restraints were adjustable for height; they also had extendable cushions to improve under-thigh support. The rear seat was a split-fold type, with a folding backrest on the right-hand side that allowed long loads to be fed through from the boot.

The instrument panel was, of course, essentially the same as on other E36s, but the dials had red markings and there was an oil temperature gauge in place of the econometer found on lesser models. An external temperature gauge and on-board computer were standard, and there were M logos on the instrument binnacle and on the gearshift grip. The steering wheel was a three-spoke type unless a driver's air-bag had been specified, in which case a rather plain-looking four-spoke type was fitted. Central locking was of course

standard, and came with a de-icer feature that automatically heated all the door locks as the key was turned in one of them. The door windows were electric, but the rear vent windows came as standard without electric assistance; power operation could be had at extra cost.

Of course, there was an array of extra-cost options. Leather upholstery could be specified (although door trim cards remained resolutely standard), and power-adjustable front seats, air conditioning, cruise control, an anti-theft alarm and metallic paint were all available to those prepared to pay for them. Also available were wider rear wheels, with 8.5J rims instead of the standard 7.5J type. Fitted with the standard size 235/40ZR17 tyres, they gave the M3 Coupé a slightly crisper turn-in to bends taken at speed.

THE M3'S HEART

So much for the cosmetics and the recognition features of the M3; the Motorsport division's real work had, of course, been concentrated on the power train and the suspension.

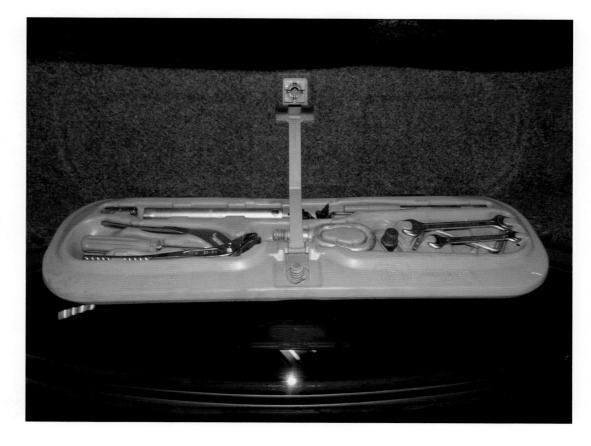

A comprehensive kit of small tools was only to be expected, and was kept in this drop-down tray under the boot lid.

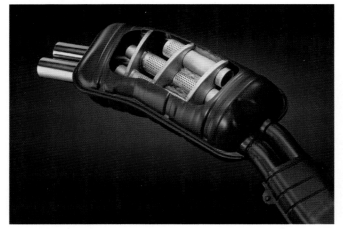

ABOVE AND BELOW: **This time the engine was a small-block 6-cylinder, with all the smoothness and punch for which BMW's sixes were already renowned. In the first E36 M3s it delivered 286PS.**

BMW were very proud of their work in creating free-flow silencers and overcoming the power restrictions of catalytic converters. This is the free-flow rear silencer developed for the E36 M3.

Central to the new M3's character was the new engine, known as an S50B30 and derived from the production M50 small-block 6-cylinder. The largest standard-production version at the time had a 2.5-litre swept volume, and the Motorsport division had enlarged the bore and lengthened the stroke to give 2990cc, usually referred to as a 3.0-litre. The basic design already incorporated four valves per cylinder, operated by twin overhead camshafts, but the M3 engine introduced a new variable valve-timing system that would only later filter its way down to the smaller engines.

This new system was called VANOS, an acronym derived from its German name of VARiable NOckenwellen Steuerung, which translates literally as variable camshaft control. (There was a brief attempt to call it VACC in English, which stood for VAriable Camshaft Control, but the name did not catch on.) VANOS operated on the inlet camshaft only, moving the camshaft forwards to retard the timing and rearwards to advance it. The results were more valve overlap for high-speed work and less for lower speeds and idling. The camshaft was moved slightly relative to its driving chain within a helical gear mounted in a housing at the front of the engine; the movement was achieved automatically by a signal from the engine management system that released oil from the main lubrication system to one side or the other of the

operating piston. Ignition and timing were adjusted to suit at the same time. The whole process was very smooth and improved fuel consumption while giving better low-speed torque and better driveability at all speeds.

In the best BMW tradition, the S50 3.0-litre was a beautifully smooth engine, with a dual-mass flywheel to improve that smoothness even more. The Bosch DME 3.3 management system had been programmed specially to suit it, and twin catalytic converters (serving three cylinders each) in the exhaust were standard. With crackle-black top covers carrying the legend 'M Power' in raised letters, the engine was carefully presented, too. With a 7,250rpm red line, it developed 286PS at 7,000rpm and 314Nm (232lb ft) at 3,600rpm – vastly more than even the most powerful versions of the 4-cylinder engine in the E30 M3. Better yet, almost all of that maximum torque was available from 3,600rpm to 5,900rpm, which gave a superbly linear delivery of thrust.

This time around, there were no uncomfortable dog-leg racing gearboxes. BMW knew that their target customers for the M3 wanted ease of driving, not difficult unfamiliarity. So the S50 engine drove through a version of the latest close-ratio, five-speed gearbox, with a direct top gear. There was enough torque for the car to pull a fairly high final drive of 3.15:1, which of course helped with fuel economy,

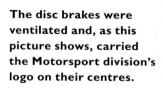

The disc brakes were ventilated and, as this picture shows, carried the Motorsport division's logo on their centres.

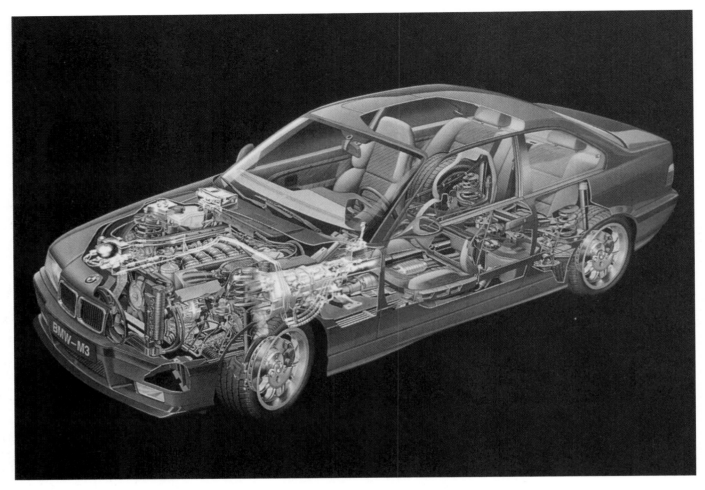

This cutaway drawing of the E36 M3 Coupé gives a very clear impression that all the interest lay under the bonnet.

and a 25 per cent limited-slip differential came as standard to control wheelspin.

Needless to say, the Motorsport division had not been content with the standard E36 suspension set-up. Most obvious was that the whole car had been lowered by 30mm (1.2in) as compared to a standard E36 Coupé. There were new progressive-rate springs, while modified front track arms gave more steering castor and there were thicker rear control arms. Both front and rear anti-roll bars were thicker than standard, and there were stronger spring plates, stronger stub axles and reinforced steering knuckles. Bigger wheel bearings came from the 8 Series coupés, and the dampers were 10 per cent stiffer than those in the optional uprated M-Technic suspension for standard cars.

The power-assisted steering was speed sensitive and reduced assistance at higher speeds. The brakes were larger than standard, too, ventilated front and rear and featuring a larger master cylinder and a retuned ABS system as standard.

As for performance, it was simply sensational for a readily-available showroom model in 1992. The M3 Coupé could hit 60mph from rest in just 5.4 seconds and would go on to 250km/h (155mph), a speed restricted by a limiter in the engine management system. BMW and other German manufacturers were at the time working to a voluntary restraint agreement, which had set maximum speeds at this level. Even so, the UK magazine *Autocar* managed to get 162mph from an M3 Coupé, apparently straight out of the box.

RHD AND US-MODEL M3 COUPÉS

The exclusively LHD availability of the E30 M3 had certainly been a hindrance to sales in RHD countries, and BMW had no intention of making the same mistake again. Even so, RHD M3s did not become available immediately but gradually reached their target markets in 1992 and 1993. South Africa was one of the first to receive them, beginning in November 1992; these cars were slightly less powerful than the European models because they were tuned to accept the lower-octane 91 RON petrol that was more or less universal in South Africa. The UK market – an important one for the M3 – did not receive any cars until May 1993.

Even more important for the M3 was the US market, and BMW took their time to get the car right before releasing it here. The first US-model M3 Coupés were built in November 1993, but the model was not announced until January 1994 and in practice cars did not become available before the spring. (In the meantime, BMW Canada managed to import some European-specification cars under a special and unique agreement, as explained in Chapter 5.) Then from early 1995 the USA was treated to a model that sounded to European enthusiasts like a contradiction in terms – an M3 with an automatic gearbox.

The US-model M3 had a very special engine of its own. Known as the S50B30US type, the American engine had the same swept volume as its European equivalent but had a different cylinder head that was much closer in specification to that used in the 325i engine. Most obviously perhaps, the cylinders did not have the individual throttle bodies that characterized the European engines. This was part of a suite of changes that had been brought about for two reasons. The first was that the European-specification engine would not pass Federal exhaust emissions regulations in its standard form, and the second was the US demand for an automatic gearbox.

This rear view of a US-specification E36 M3 Coupé shows the high-mounted third brake light that was standard for some markets, including the USA.

This demand for an automatic option caused BMW a few headaches. The major problem was that none of the automatic gearboxes available to them at the time could handle the wide rev range of the M3 engine, which delivered its peak power at 7,400rpm. So the only option that the Motorsport division's engineers had was to reduce the rev range. This was the main reason why the US-model M3 engine was much less powerful than the European version. As first released, it had just 243PS (240bhp to Americans) at a low-sounding 6,000rpm, together with 305Nm (225lb ft) at 4,250rpm. The US-model M3 would always remain the only E36 M3 variant to have an automatic gearbox, and it came with a five-speed unit by ZF, which was matched by a lower 3.23:1 final drive to restore lost acceleration.

There were other changes in specification to suit US tastes. So the cars had the standard E36 econometer instead of an oil pressure gauge; they came with twin airbags and air conditioning as standard; and they had a third brake light mounted behind the rear screen glass. Optional, at extra cost, were an electric sunroof, heated seats, onboard computer, cruise control and a rear spoiler. Leather upholstery and metallic paint were no-cost options from the beginning.

Early 1995 brought a new range of options for both manual and automatic derivatives of the M3 in the USA. The cars could now be ordered with the Double-Spoke alloy wheels that had made their debut in spring 1994 on the M3 Convertible for Europe (see below). More important for many buyers, though, was the optional Luxury Package. Some of its contents really were luxurious, but others were cosmetic addenda that allowed buyers to make their cars look different from other M3s. At the front, the Luxury Package brought the European-specification M3 Saloon spoiler with its less pronounced lip and horizontal slots. (The Saloon is discussed later.) There were plainer, less sculpted sill panels and M Contour II five-spoke alloy wheels.

On the inside, the Luxury Package added the power-adjustable sports seats already available in European Convertibles, with leather upholstery and leather door-trim panels. A front armrest, walnut wood trim and chrome door handles lent extra character to the cabin, while a cruise control and on-board computer brought additional functional equipment.

CONVERTIBLES AND SALOONS, 1994

No one was very surprised when an M3 Convertible was announced in spring 1994. The convertible E36 had been

ABOVE AND OPPOSITE TOP: **The Convertible, too, was positively suave in its appearance. BMW had concluded that this was what M3 buyers really wanted. Note also the different wheels compared with Coupé derivatives.**

announced during 1993 and it could only be a matter of time before an M3 derivative followed to pick up where the E30 M3 Convertible had left off in 1991.

Though the M3 Convertible looked like a Coupé with the roof removed, there was actually much more to it than that. The E36 Convertible had been engineered separately from the Coupé, and as a result had ended up with some dimensional differences. Extensive underbody reinforcement had led to a minor increase in the wheelbase. The windscreen frame was heavily reinforced to act as a rollover bar, and additional rollover bars sprang up from behind the rear seats if the car tilted past a certain point. All this helped to make an M3 Convertible some 80kg (176lb) heavier than its Coupé equivalent.

The Convertible roof was power-operated, as shown in this composite picture.

Like all the E36 convertibles, the M3 had a superbly made soft top. As the flagship model, it came with the electro-hydraulic power operation that was an extra-cost option on lesser models. All the driver had to do was to release a twist grip on the windscreen header rail, press a button on the centre console, and the top would fold itself away neatly with a thud under its metal tonneau cover behind the rear seats. Erecting the top was just as simple, and for those who really preferred a solid roof during the winter, a removable hardtop was available as an option – and at vast expense, which ensured it would remain rare.

The M3 Convertible shared its 'crossover' pattern side sills with the Coupé, but had a more discreet front air dam with a less pronounced lip. It had forged and polished 17-inch M-Style Double-Spoke alloy wheels and always had the wider 8.5J rims at the rear. Nappa leather upholstery was standard, the rear seat had no split-fold function and all seat backs carried a tricolour label. Electric windows all round were standard, and all could be raised or lowered together by a single switch. In addition, they dropped automatically to give clearance when the convertible top was being closed.

Later in 1994, the M3 model range in Europe was swelled to three when an M3 Saloon was announced. Though at first sight a four-door M3 seemed like a contradiction in terms, there was actually a very good reason for its existence. The E34 M5 four-door saloon was due to go out of production during 1995, and BMW would not replace it until 1998, when an M5 derivative of the forthcoming E39 5 Series would be introduced. That left a gap of around three years when there would be no 'businessman's express' saloon from the Motorsport division on the market, and so an M3 Saloon was developed to fill that gap.

The power train of the M3 Saloon was the same as that in the Coupé and Convertible and, although the car was

The Saloon version was just as subtle as the Coupé and Convertible, and again featured a different wheel design. It was essentially intended to hold the fort while BMW readied their new M5 for production.

Kick plates carried the M3 logo on both front and rear doors of the M3 Saloon.

some 15kg (33lb) heavier than the equivalent Coupé, it was just as fast. However, this was a car that might actually be used to carry four passengers on a regular basis (the cramped rear seat of the Coupé made that impossible unless it was occupied by children), and so its suspension was tuned to give a rather softer ride. The Saloon also had the more discreet front apron from the Convertible, while rather less overt side sills helped tone down the appearance for its intended customers.

Nevertheless, BMW knew enough about 'surprise and delight' features by now and wisely endowed the car with unique five-spoke alloy wheels. As an option, the cars could also have the M-Style Double-Spoke wheels of the Convertible, although in a plain and not polished finish. Wood trim on the centre console, shift grip and door pulls was also standard, along with chromed door-release handles, and the rear seat was a split-fold type. Like the Coupés by this stage, the Saloons could be ordered with a rear sunblind and an M rear wing spoiler, both of course at extra cost.

These were the distinctive five-spoke wheels of the M3 Saloon. Note the Motorsport logo below the BMW badge in the centre.

By late 1994, the full three-model M3 range was in place.

THE M3 EVOLUTION, 1995

As with all performance-oriented cars, it was important for BMW to keep the M3 ahead of potential rivals, and so the model took on a more powerful engine along with some cosmetic upgrades in October 1995. This second-generation E36 M3 was generally known as the M3 Evolution, borrowing a name from the racing 'evolutions' of the original E30 M3.

It was in fact introduced in stages, the Coupé receiving the upgrades first, the Saloon in November 1995 and the Convertible following in February 1996. RHD cars for the UK also became available that month, but there would be none for South Africa until September that year. The last of 748 3.0-litre M3 Coupés had been built for that country in 1994, and availability resumed in September 1996 when the

The boot was wholly practical. This is on a UK-market Evolution Saloon.

TOP: **Though certainly not aggressive, the M3's front spoiler was distinctively different from that of the standard E36. This one is on an Evolution Saloon.**

BELOW: **The centre stack of the M3's dashboard had the same neat design as the standard E36, although it contained a generally higher level of equipment. Note also the gate pattern and M logo on the gearshift grip.**

Evolution Coupés began to come off assembly lines at the BMW plant in Rosslyn, near Pretoria in Gauteng province. Local assembly began with 168 cars shipped out in part-built form (SKD or Semi-Knocked Down) and then progressed to a further 272 shipped in kit form (CKD or Completely Knocked Down) for more demanding local assembly. All 440 cars appear to have been sold as 1997 models.

Central to the Evolution was of course that new engine, generally known as a 3.2-litre type. In fact there were two different versions, one for Europe and the other for the USA. Still based on the M50 small-block 'six', it was known as an S50B32 in European trim and an S52B32US in US form.

The European versions boasted 321PS at 7,400rpm and 350Nm (258lb ft) at 3,250rpm, both figures being considerably higher than for the older 3.0-litre engine. As before, a nearly flat torque curve running upwards from 3,250rpm ensured rapid response to the accelerator at high speeds. The 0–100km/h (0–62mph) sprint was achievable in just 5.5 seconds, and although the cars came with a limiter in the engine management system that restricted maximum speed to 250km/h (155mph), the Motorsport division claimed that 290km/h (180mph) was realistic with the limiter disabled.

The major dimensional change from the previous engine was to the stroke, and even though the bore was also very

slightly enlarged, the result was an under-square engine – most unusual for BMW at the time. The European swept volume was 3201cc, and the engine now boasted double-VANOS, giving automatic adjustment of both inlet and exhaust camshafts. To control this, the Motorsport division had developed its own engine-management system in tandem with specialists Siemens, and this was known as the MSS 50 type.

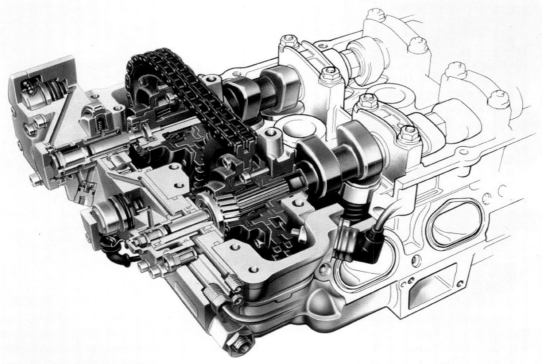

Adding a variable camshaft to the exhaust side of the engine improved power and torque still further. This is the double-VANOS system of the later, or Evolution, cars. On the black-and-white picture, sections of the housing have been cut away to show how the system works.

Bigger inlet valves, lightweight pistons and a reworked exhaust manifold were among the other changes, and the con rods were now graphite coated to reduce friction. An improved dual-mass flywheel and modified vibration damper ensured that the engine was as silky smooth as BMW sixes were expected to be, and a second oil pump was employed to make doubly sure that there was adequate lubrication when the car was cornering hard. Though few customers probably cared, the engine actually used less fuel than its predecessor too.

Most of these innovations were also present in the US Evolution engine, which had a shorter stroke and a swept volume of just 3152cc. Still under-square, it had the same 10.5:1 compression ratio but was once again considerably less powerful than its European equivalent. Power was barely more than from the 3.0-litre engine, with 243bhp at 6,000rpm, and torque of 325Nm (240lb ft) at 3,800rpm was an improvement mainly in that it was produced at lower engine revolutions than before. When allied to the optional (and still US-only) automatic gearbox, the torque figure was reduced to give smoother changes.

The availability of an automatic gearbox was not the only other difference between European and US Evolution models. European cars now came with a six-speed manual gearbox, while the US models still had the earlier five-speed type. However, both manual and automatic cars for the USA now shared the lower 3.23:1 final drive for improved acceleration.

The six-speed gearbox was derived from the one seen in the E34 M5, and essentially added an overdrive top gear to the four close intermediate ratios and direct-drive fifth gear. Six-speed gearboxes were already quite common in

Though undeniably purposeful in appearance, the E36 M3 Evolution remained quite subtle. The clear lenses for the rear turn indicators are obvious in this picture of a UK-market example.

Evolution models used clear lenses for the front indicators and side repeaters.

racing machinery, and had been seen in some of the E30 M3 track cars, so there was status appeal in having one in the M3. Nevertheless, it appears that one of the driving forces behind the change to a six-speed gearbox was, in fact, drive-by noise regulations in some European countries. The M3 was quieter at full chat in overdrive sixth than in direct-drive fifth!

The Evolution Coupés and Convertibles all had new springs and dampers in their M-Sport suspension, although the Saloons retained their softer suspension (which was also optional on other E36s), and all three models had increased front-wheel castor to improve straight-line stability. Specially developed for the cars was a new ABS system, which had resulted from collaboration between the Motorsport division and Alfred Teves GmbH; it was known as the Teves MkIV system. The European cars had floating-caliper brakes, too, as on the most recent M5, but the US cars retained their older brakes. The M5 had also donated its 25 per cent limited-slip differential, and all the Evolution cars combined this with an ASC+T electronic traction-control system (the letters stood for Automatische Stabilitäts Control+Traktion, which translates as 'automatic stability control and traction'). Quicker steering was another improvement.

Cosmetic changes were surprisingly limited at this stage,

perhaps because a further facelift was planned for 1996. However, the Evolution cars were readily recognizable by a matt black grille in the front air dam (on Coupés and Convertibles) and by horizontal bars in the grille aperture (on Saloons). They had clear indicator lenses and a third brake lamp like that that available for some time on US cars. The US cars, however, retained amber indicator lenses to meet local regulations. Saloons now had the crossover-pattern sills already standard on other models.

The Evolution Saloons had a new design of sill, without the 'crossover' feature seen before.

There were also some changes to the alloy wheel line-up. Coupé models now had ten-spoke M-Style Double-Spoke II wheels, while Convertibles had five-spoke M-Style Double Spokes. Saloons had five-spoke M-Contour II wheels, but the polished M-Style Double Spokes of the Convertibles were optional. The standard tyre combination for all three models was 225/45R17s on the front with 245/40R17s on the rear, which posed a problem for the spare. In practice, the spare was always supplied with the smaller tyre size, as used on the front wheels.

Other changes were less obvious. Important, though invisible, was the standardization of lighter aluminium door skins for the Coupé and Convertible models. Air conditioned cars now normally came with the Automatic Climate Control system, where the required temperature was entered and the system worked out how to maintain it by blending outside, heated and cooled air as appropriate. When Coupés were ordered with leather upholstery, the door cards were now also in leather. Convertibles had leather as standard, together with a rear seat armrest, and burr walnut trim on the centre console, shift grip and door pulls. They also had metallic paint as standard. Saloons came with leather uphol-

stery and a rear armrest as standard, plus a front centre armrest, electric windows and the wood trim.

Finally, there were some special features for the US cars. They all came with wiring installed so that a CD changer or a mobile phone could simply be plugged in and used. The standard audio system was an AM/FM stereo-cassette with RDS, and when the optional Harman/Kardon system was ordered, it came with a six-CD changer. The engines were fitted with an EWS rolling-code immobilizer to guard against theft, and for similar reasons the central locking came with a double-lock feature, while locking the driver's door now

TOP: **The steering wheel had the usual tricolour stitching. Note also the key fob here.**

BELOW: **The Saloon models brought additional practicality. Seat belts were neatly arranged so that both straps were in the middle of the car.**

automatically closed all the electric windows. There was also a crash sensor that automatically activated the hazard warning lights, unlocked all the doors and switched on the interior lights in the event of a collision.

THE FACELIFT AND SMG, 1996

Changes elsewhere in the BMW range prompted the next stage in the life of the E36 models. The catalyst was the introduction of the new E39 5 Series saloons in 1996. The 1995 E38 7 Series had a subtly revised front-end design that was more rounded than before, and once this had filtered down to the new mid-range saloons, it made the existing 3 Series design look outdated. So from September 1996 the M3, along with all other E36 models then in production, took on a new front-end design with a more rounded twin-kidney grille that had more substantial bright frames. There was a new panel around the headlamps as well.

BMW seized the opportunity to introduce several other upgrades at the same time. These included a new M-Sport three-spoke airbag steering wheel, mercifully better-looking than the old four-spoke design. Twin airbags were probably

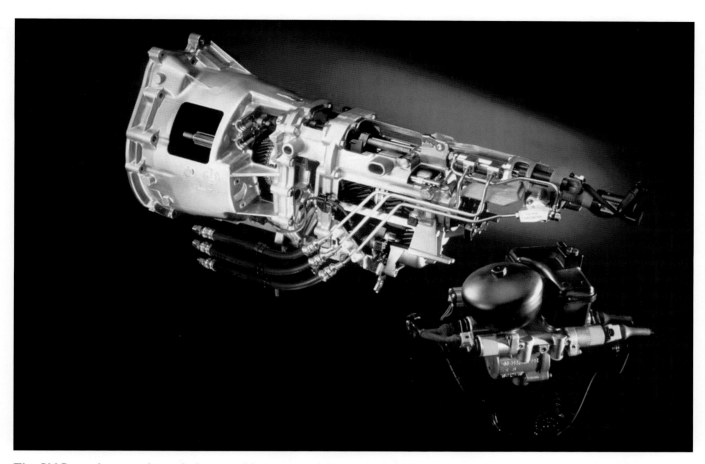

The **SMG** gearbox was intended to combine two-pedal control with racing-style fast gear changes. This press picture of an SMG-equipped car being 'maxed' helped to demonstrate that top-end performance was just as good as ever.

THE SOUTH AFRICAN CKD CARS

As noted in the main text, BMW assembled a number of M3 saloons from CKD kits for the South African market at its Rosslyn plant near Pretoria.

These cars were broadly similar to the RHD European models but had a low-compression engine to cope with the poor quality of South African petrol. The lower value of 10.5:1 was achieved by using special pistons, and their outputs were quoted as 310PS at 7,400rpm and 340Nm (251lb ft) at 3,250rpm. None of the South African cars was fitted with the SMG gearbox.

The cars were built with a high level of standard equipment, which included forged M Double-Spoke alloy wheels, M3 GT-style front 'splitters', electric sunroof, extended Nappa leather upholstery, electric front seats, rear sunshade, automatic climate control, cruise control and an on-board computer. They shared some colours and trims with German-built cars, but also had some unique ones, as the tables below show.

Paints

Shared colours	BMW code	Unique colours	BMW code
Alpine White III	300	Aegean Blue metallic	336
Arctic Silver metallic	309	Avus Blue metallic	276
Bright Red	314	British Racing Green	312
Cosmos Black metallic	303	Daytona Violet metallic	299
Dakar Yellow II	337	Santorini Blue II	327
Titanium Silver metallic	354		

Upholstery

There were three choices of upholstery colour, and in all cases the cars had 'extended' Nappa leather. The Black and Mulberry options were shared with German-built M3s, but Champagne Extended Nappa leather (coded L7CN) was unique to South African models.

standardized for all markets at the same time, having previously been an extra-cost option. US cars took on new side running lights at this stage too, but US models did not all receive the new steering wheel, which was fitted only to Convertibles for that market.

There was a further significant change in mid-season, but for the European market only. This was the introduction of a new Sequential Manual Gearbox as an extra-cost option. The new gearbox had actually been announced in July 1996, but it did not reach the M3 until March 1997 and it would be March 1998 before it became available in the UK. Inevitably known as the SMG type, the new gearbox had six speeds with a servo-actuated clutch.

Its electronic control system depended on a shift lever similar to that of an automatic, but with two overlapping 'gates'. Moving the lever to the left-hand gate selected the fully automatic 'Economy' mode, but moving it to the right or 'Sports' gate gave sequential up or down changes under manual control. Moving the lever forwards in that right-hand gate gave an upchange, and moving it backwards gave a downchange. The changes were slick and fast, and the system incorporated checks and overrides to prevent damage caused by inexpert use.

THE LAST CARS, 1997 AND 1998

The 1998 model year that began in September 1997 was the last full season for the E36 M3 worldwide although some markets continued to take new M3s into the 1999 model year.

There were a few changes for the 1998 models, notably a reversion to steel door skins for the Coupé and Convertible. Exactly why this was done is not clear; perhaps there

The 50,000th M3 was delivered to the Bavarian Police for motorway patrol duties.

had been problems with the aluminium panels becoming dented, or perhaps there had simply been a cost-saving drive on production at Regensburg. There had been side airbags as an option on Saloons from spring 1997, and these now became standard on all three models from September 1997. An illuminated shift grip also became standard on all three variants of M3.

There was a change in the marketing of options on US models in September 1997 too. Leather upholstery became standard on Coupés, and the Luxury Package was discontinued. Instead, most of its components became available as separate items, and the cruise control, on-board computer and M-Contour wheels could now be ordered individually. Saloons already had power-adjustable seats as standard, but these became extra-cost options on Coupés and Convertibles as well, while extra cup holders – an American favourite – became a no-cost dealer-fit option. The 1998-model US Coupés could also be ordered with a 'two-way moon roof', which translated as a clear glass tilt-and-slide sunroof that was, naturally, electrically operated. All the 1998 US models came with a front armrest too.

The Saloon models were the first ones to end production,

in anticipation of the new E39 M5's arrival – announced at the Geneva Show in February 1998, it actually became available the following October. BMW arranged for the last saloon off the line to become the ceremonial 50,000th M3 (whether it was exactly that is probably immaterial), and after the ceremony on 12 December 1997 it was handed over to the Bavarian Police. The car became an Autobahn patrol unit, and was modified to suit its new task. The luggage capacity was increased (probably by modifying the rear seat), and firearms supports were mounted under the roof lining. Two interior mirrors were fitted, along with police radios and an electrical power take-off. The vehicle was finished in the standard white and green of German police cars, and a light array with public address system was mounted on the roof.

Only right at the end of production, in mid-1998, did the US M3 Coupés get the latest three-spoke airbag steering wheel that was already standard on Convertibles. Coupé production then ended in late 1998, although Convertible production continued at a low level and primarily for the US market until December 1999. This final period was marked by some final farewell editions in various countries, but by the end of 1999 the E36 M3 was no more.

THE STILLBORN M3 COMPACT

BMW expanded its mainstream E36 range in 1994 to include a two-box 'Compact' model, which was essentially a two-door saloon that had been shortened behind the rear wheels. It was BMW's first entry into the 'hot hatchback' market that was dominated at the time by the Volkswagen Golf.

This was the one and only M3 Compact.

To gauge public reaction to the idea of an M3 Compact, BMW Motorsport built a prototype during 1996, and presented it to the German magazine *auto, motor und sport* for the magazine's fiftieth anniversary. The car was described and tested for the June issue of the magazine.

No production followed. The single prototype had a standard Evolution 321PS 3201cc engine and five-speed gearbox, with the rear axle from an M Roadster (which was based on the Z3 two-seater). It was finished in red with a black cloth-and-Amaretta suede interior and had Amaretta trim on the steering wheel and shift grip. There were red four-point belts on its Recaro sports bucket seats. The wheels were the five-spoke type from the contemporary M3 Saloon, and the car was 230mm (9in) shorter than a standard M3, as well as 150kg (331lb) lighter. Maximum speed was limited to 250km/h (155mph) in the usual way, and the 0–100km/h (0–62mph) sprint took 5.2 seconds.

COLOURS AND TRIMS FOR E36 M3 MODELS

Paint

Colour	BMW paint code	Colour	BMW paint code
Alpine White III	300	Dakar Yellow	337
Arctic Silver	309	Estoril Blue	335
Boston Green	275	Fern Green	386
Bright Red	314	Imola Red	405
Byzanz (blue)	355	Techno Violet	299
Cosmos Black	303	Titanium Silver	354

Notes:

(1) Byzanz was available only on 1997-model Saloons (built between September 1996 and August 1997).

(2) The paint range changed in March 1998: Titanium Silver replaced Arctic Silver, Fern Green replaced Boston Green, and Imola Red was made available only on the M3 Evo Individual cars (see Chapter 5).

Convertible tops

The fabric covering of the convertible top was always Black (code 388), with the following exceptions:

Estoril Blue cars could have Dark Blue (code 391) tops when a Light Grey interior was specified.

Fern Green cars could have Dark Green (code 392) tops with all interior colours except Sand Beige.

Interior

Early cars could have upholstery in M-Cross cloth with Amaretta side bolsters. This was discontinued for the US market in September 1997 but remained available in some other territories, including Canada.

The following options were available with Nappa leather upholstery.

Colour	BMW trim code	Colour	BMW trim code
Black	N5SW	Modena Natur	N5AY
Light Grey	N5TT	Mulberry	N5MQ
Magma	N5AX	Sand Beige	N5SN

On US-specification M3s, Magma and Mulberry Nappa leather were initially available only as part of the Luxury Package option. They became standard production options in their own right from November 1997; on cars for Canada, both these colours and Modena Natur were discontinued in August 1997.

Sand Beige leather was introduced for the USA from September 1998.

E36 M3 SPECIFICATIONS

Engines:
3.0-litre
Type S50B30 6-cylinder petrol
2990cc (86mm × 85.8mm)
Twin overhead camshafts, chain-driven
VANOS variable valve timing on inlet camshaft
Four valves per cylinder
Seven-bearing crankshaft
Compression ratio 10.8:1
Bosch Motronic M3.3 engine-management system
Catalytic converter standard (three-way converter with twin
    Lambda probes)
286PS at 7,000rpm
240PS at 6,000rpm (US models)
314Nm (232lb ft) at 3,600rpm
305Nm (225lb ft) at 4,250rpm (US models)

3.2-litre (Evolution models for Europe)
Type S50B32 6-cylinder petrol
3201cc (86.4mm × 91mm)
Twin overhead camshafts, chain-driven
VANOS variable valve timing on inlet and exhaust camshafts
Four valves per cylinder
Seven-bearing crankshaft
Compression ratio 11.3:1
BMW MSS 50 engine-management system
Catalytic converter standard (three-way converter with twin
    Lambda probes)
321PS at 7,400rpm
350Nm (258lb ft) at 3,250rpm

3.2-litre (Evolution models for USA)
Type S52B32US 6-cylinder petrol
3152cc (86.4mm × 89.6mm)
Twin overhead camshafts, chain-driven
VANOS variable valve timing on inlet and exhaust camshafts
Four valves per cylinder
Seven-bearing crankshaft
Compression ratio 10.5:1
BMW MSS 50 engine-management system
Catalytic converter standard (three-way converter with twin
    Lambda probes)
243PS at 6,000rpm

320Nm (236lb ft) at 3,800rpm for manual models
305Nm (225lb ft) for automatic models

Transmission:
Five-speed ZF manual gearbox on 1992–95 models and all
    US cars
Ratios 4.20:1, 2.49:1, 1.66:1, 1.24:1, 1.00:1; reverse 3.89:1
Six-speed ZF manual gearbox on Evolution models for
    Europe
Ratios 4.23:1, 2.51:1, 1.67:1, 1.23:1, 1.00:1, 0.83:1; reverse
    3.89:1
Five-speed ZF 5HP18 automatic gearbox optional on US
    Evolution models
Ratios 3.67:1, 2.00:1, 1.41:1, 1.00:1, 0.74:1; reverse 4.10:1

Axle ratio:
Standard   3.15:1 on 1992–95 models for Europe
            3.23:1 on all US cars and on Evolution models

Suspension, steering and brakes:
Front suspension with MacPherson struts, coil springs, Boge
    gas dampers and anti-roll bar
Rear suspension: Coupé models with 'Z-axle', consisting of
                  semi-trailing arms, separate springs and
                  Boge gas dampers, and anti-roll bar.
                  Convertible and Saloon models with
                  multi-link system, coil springs Boge gas
                  dampers and anti-roll bar
Rack-and-pinion steering with speed-sensitive variable ratio
    and standard power assistance; ratio variable between
    15.4:1 and 19.8:1
Ventilated disc brakes all round, 315mm (12.4in) on front
    wheels and 312mm (12.3in) on rear wheels; twin hydraulic
    circuits; ABS standard

Dimensions:
Overall length: 4,433mm (174.5in) for standard models
                 4,521mm (178.0in) for M3 Lightweight
Overall width: 1,710mm (67.3in) for Coupés and
                 Convertibles
                 1,699mm (66.9in) for Saloons
Overall height: 1,336mm (52.6in) for Coupés
                 1,366mm (53.8in) for Saloons
                 1,340mm (52.8in) for Convertibles (top
                 down)

E36 M3 SPECIFICATIONS *continued*

Wheelbase:	2,700mm (106.3in) for Coupés and Saloons
	2,710mm (106.7in) for Convertibles
Front track:	1,422mm (56.0in)
Rear track:	1,444mm (56.9in)

Wheels and tyres:

7.5J × 17 five-stud alloy wheels with 235/40 ZR 17 tyres, 1992–95 models

7.5J × 17 five-stud alloy wheels with 225/45R17 front tyres and 245/40R17 rear tyres, Evolution models

Optional 8.5J × 17 five-stud alloy wheels on rear, with 235/40 ZR 17 tyres, 1992–95 models

Unladen weights:

Coupé	1,460kg/3,219lb
Convertible	1,560kg/3,439lb
Saloon	1,535kg/3,384lb (kerb weight)

PERFORMANCE FIGURES FOR E36 M3 MODELS

Coupé	0–60mph	5.4 sec	
	Maximum	261km/h (162mph)	(*Autocar* figures)
Convertible	0–60mph	5.7 sec	
	Maximum	250km/h (155mph)	(*Autocar* figures)
Saloon	0–60mph	5.5 sec	
	Maximum	251km/h (156mph)	(*Autocar* figures)
Evolution	0–60mph	5.4 sec	
	Maximum	250km/h (155mph)	(BMW figures)

All cars had a speed limiter that theoretically limited maximum speed to 250km/h (155mph).

E36 M3 VIN CODES AND SEQUENCES

All E36 M3 models have a 17-digit Vehicle Identification Number (VIN). This consists of a ten-digit prefix and a seven-digit serial number. The serial number may consist of six numbers or a combination of letters and numbers.

A theoretical example would be:

WBSBF9100SEH76543

which decodes as shown below. Alternatives for each position are shown in the right-hand column.

WBS	BMW Motorsport GmbH, Munich
BF	3.0-litre Coupé
	BG = 3.2-litre (Evolution) Coupé
	BJ = 3.0-litre Convertible (Europe)
	BK = Evolution Convertible and US 3.0-litre Convertible
	CB = 3.0-litre Saloon
	CD = Evolution Saloon and US 3.0-litre auto Saloon
91	LHD, European specification
	92 = RHD, European specification
	93 = LHD, US specification
	98 = RHD, South African, SKD and CKD
	99 = LHD, M3 GT
	03 = LHD, US specification automatic
0	Standard placeholder code on European cars
	0 = Manual safety belts (on US cars)
	1 = Belts and driver's airbag (on US cars)
	2 = Belts and twin airbags (on US cars)
0	Standard place-holder code on European cars
	Check digit (1–9, or X) on US cars
S	1995 model year
	T = 1996 V = 1998
	U = 1997 W = 1999
76543	Serial number
	(For more on these, *see below*.)

E36 M3 VIN CODES AND SEQUENCES *continued*

Serial numbers:

Model	Build dates	Serial numbers
BF03	12/1995 to 01/1996	No details available
BF91	03/1992 to 11/1994	JC30000 to JC39999
	04/1992 to 07/1995	JF80000 to JF81438
BF92	03/1993 to 06/1995	EA66000 to EA 68999
	1995	EA85000 to EA85223
BF93	11/1993 to 12/1995	EH00000 to EH06538
BF98	09/1993 to 05/1994	No details available
BF99	12/1994 to 06/1995	EA40000 to EA 40355
BG91	03/1995 to 12/1998	EW35000 to EW 35020
BG92	01/1996 to 12/1998	No details available
BG93	03/1996 to 04/1999	No details available
BJ91	11/1993 to 07/1994	EE40000 to EE40577
	08/1994 to 08/1995	EE40600 to EE41428
BJ92	03/1994 to 07/1994	ES85000 to ES 85164
	09/1994 to 08/1995	ES85200 to ES85608

Model	Build dates	Serial numbers
BK03	03/1998 to 08/1999	No details available
BK91	02/1996 to 08/1998	No details available
BK92	02/1996 to 07/1999	No details available
BK93	03/1998 to 08/1999	No details available
CB91	06/1994 to 07/1995	EW20000 to EW20886
CB92	10/1994 to 07/1995	EW30000 to EW30337
CD03	07/1996 to 05/1998	No details available
CD91	11/1995 to 01/1998	EW73000 to EW73017
CD92	01/1996 to 12/1997	No details available
CD93	07/1996 to 05/1998	No details available
CD98	11/1996 to 10/1998	No details available

The build dates shown here are from the best available sources. Serial numbers for the various models are shown where these are known.

The VIN was stamped into the bulkhead of the car and was visible with the bonnet open. More visibly, it could also be seen through the base of the windscreen on the opposite side.

PRODUCTION FIGURES FOR E36 M3 MODELS

These figures are for calendar years. Note that in 1995 production switched to M3 Evolution models, and that the 1995 totals therefore embrace both types of M3 built that year.

	Coupé	Convertible	Saloon	KD *	Total
1992	470			50	520
1993	6080	3		632	6715
1994	9289	1118	288	66	10,761
1995	9828	860	1282	0	11,970
1996	6896	1248	3639	168	11,951
1997	**	**	**	**	11,933
1998	**	**	**	**	6118

*   KD (Knocked Down, or kit form) assembly was only ever done in South Africa and began in November 1992. Assembly was of SKD (Semi-Knocked-Down) kits between 1992 and 1994; there was then a break of one year, and assembly progressed in 1996 to CKD (Completely Knocked Down).

**   Individual model breakdowns for these years are not currently available. Note also that the total production figures are for the 1997 and 1998 model years, not calendar years. The 1997 figures therefore duplicate a proportion of those shown for the 1996 calendar year. Convertible production, mainly for the USA, continued into 1999.

M3 Coupé, 1992–99

Model		Production	Total	Type total
3.0-litre	LHD	1992–95	11,284	
	RHD	1993–95	3,112	14,396
M3 GT	LHD	1994–95	356	
	RHD	1994	50	406
US manual	LHD	1994–95	8,515	
automatic	LHD	1994–95	1,705	10,220
South Africa	RHD	1992–95	748	748
Evolution	LHD	1995–98	5,190	
	RHD	1995–98	1,925	7,115
US 3.2-litre	LHD	1995–98	6,299	6,299
Grand total				**39,184**

M3 Convertible, 1993–99

Model		Production	Total	Type total
3.0-litre	LHD	1993–95	1,403	
	RHD	1994–95	572	1,975
Evolution	LHD	1995–98	1,290	
	RHD	1995–98	1,085	2,375
US manual	LHD	1998–99	12	
automatic	LHD	1998–99	2	14
Grand total				**4,364**

M3 saloon, 1993–99

Model		Production	Total	Type total
3.0-litre	LHD	1994–95	888	
	RHD	1994–95	415	1,303
Evolution	LHD	1995–97	1,295	
	RHD	1995–97	694	1,989
S. Africa SKD	RHD	1996	168	
CKD	RHD	1997	272	440
US manual	LHD	1996–98	3,223	
automatic	LHD	1996–98	3,162	6,385
Grand total				**10,117**

CHAPTER FIVE

DRIVING, BUYING AND SPECIAL EDITIONS OF THE E36 M3

By the time of the E36 M3, BMW was very much aware of the value of limited editions in generating showroom traffic. As these applied to the M3, however, they were not simply variations on the standard specification created by putting together packages of options from the standard sales catalogue. Almost all the special editions of the E36 M3 had some direct link with motor sport: several were in effect 'homologation specials'.

Sadly, changes in FIA regulations kept the E36 M3 out of many high-profile European racing events although the cars were most certainly active in those events where their engine size did not debar them from entry. Meanwhile, in the USA the E36 M3 was central to BMW's national racing campaign.

The special-edition cars built between 1994 and 1999 were all market-specific rather than globally available. So there were specials for Europe (including the UK), specials for Germany only, specials for the USA, specials for Canada and specials for Australia.

1994: THE M3 EURO-SPEC CANADIAN EDITION

No M3s were available in any part of North America before the 1995 model year, but BMW Canada were able to steal a march on their counterparts in the USA during 1994 by taking advantage of a unique trade agreement between Canada and the European Union. This agreement stated that any car that met regulations obtaining in one of the countries that was party to the agreement could also be sold in the other countries.

So BMW Canada seized their chance and imported a total of forty-five M3 Coupés, which thus became the first E36 M3 models of any kind in North America. Legend has it that all forty-five had found buyers within three days of going on sale.

The cars were essentially European-specification M3s but with the daytime running lights required in Canada and a third brake light mounted behind the rear window glass. They were given added appeal by a numbered, engraved limited-edition plaque in the glove box and a special leather case for the owner's manuals, which also carried the limited edition number.

Canada then received no more M3s until the arrival of the 1997-model US-specification cars.

1994: THE M3 GT

The M3 GT was a homologation special that allowed the car to compete in European FIA GT Class II, IMSA GT and international long-distance races. The first six prototypes were built in December 1994, and the production cars were built between February and June 1995. There were 350 examples with left-hand drive, and a further fifty with right-hand drive for the UK.

The cars had the Coupé body shell, and all were painted in British Racing Green (BMW code 312) with a Mexico Green leather interior that included some Kevlar trim parts. They had a front air dam with splitter, a rear spoiler, and their suspension was stiffened and lowered. All examples seem to have had clear front-indicator lenses but orange lenses for the rear indicators and side repeaters.

Their engines delivered 295PS at 7,100rpm, with 323Nm (238lb ft) at 3,900rpm. Key changes from the standard 3.0-litre engine were altered camshafts and a 10.8:1 compression ratio, special ECU software, a Motorsport oil pump and a double oil pickup in a special sump.

Engine changes were a feature of 1994's M3 GT, but the British Racing Green paintwork was an aid to recognition.

The M3 GT was around 30kg (66lb) lighter than the standard M3 Coupé of the time, and had no speed limiter in its engine-management system. It was capable of a maximum 275km/h (171mph).

1994: THE M3 GT-R

The M3 GT-R was a very limited edition of which just two road-legal examples were made. It was based on the competition car that was built to compete in the 1994 ADAC German GT Cup Touring Car series.

The GT-R had a 300PS version of the standard 3.0-litre engine. Lightweight body panels and a stripped-out interior

reduced its kerb weight to 1,300kg (2,866lb). There were flared wings over 18-inch wheels with wide tyres, adjustable spoilers front and rear, and a full racing roll cage.

1994: THE M3-R

The M3-R was created to allow BMW Australia to go racing in the Australian Super Production series, where Frank Gardner's BMW M Team prepared and campaigned them. It was a limited run of fifteen cars, of which four went to the Gardner team and the remaining eleven were offered for sale to members of the public who owned a CAMS (Confederation of Australian Motor Sport) racing licence. All fifteen

Just two 'street' versions of the M3 GT-R were built. The relationship to the racing version is immediately obvious in these views.

It is unclear whether these two pictures show the same car at different times or both of the two 'street' M3 GT-R cars. The internal roll cage is immediately obvious in both. One picture shows M3 badging (and the car has been road-registered in Munich).

cars were painted in Alpine White III, with Anthracite upholstery in M cloth and Amaretta suede, and each car had an individually numbered plate mounted on the centre console.

The cars were built as standard M3 Coupés in Germany, without air conditioning and with a GT adjustable front splitter and a Class II Evolution two-part racing rear wing with flaps. They were delivered to Tony Longhurst Racing in Australia, where they were stripped of 'unnecessary equipment'.

That meant that the sound insulation, rear seat, spare wheel, tool kit, boot trim and rear interior trim were all removed; even the M3 badges disappeared. This lightened the cars by around 200kg (441lb).

There then followed a considerable degree of further modification. Engine work included a twin-rotor oil pump with dual pickups and a baffled sump, an oil restrictor in the cylinder head, AC Schnitzer cams, shorter inlet trumpets, a lightened flywheel, a remapped ECU and a cold air intake with its pickup replacing the left-hand fog light in the front air dam. These changes delivered 326PS (322bhp) at 6,000rpm with a restrictor in place; a claimed 395bhp was available without it. Torque was claimed to be 350Nm (258lb ft) at 4,400rpm.

The uprated engine drove through an AP Racing twin-plate racing clutch with heavy-duty release bearing to a 3.23:1 final drive with stronger driveshafts taken from the E31 850Ci Coupé. The M3-Rs were fitted with Australian-made King springs and Group N adjustable struts and rear spring plates. All examples had 17-inch BBS cross-spoke alloy wheels, the early ones with 7.5J rims all round but later cars with the wider 8.5J rims on the rear. Original tyres were Michelin Pilot SX 235/45ZR17s all round, and there were four-piston racing calipers from AP Racing. An FIA-approved roll cage, made in Australia by Dencar, could be bolted in as an extra-cost option.

BMW Australia claimed that an M3-R was capable of about 290km/h (180mph), and with the standard restrictor could reach 100km/h (62mph) from rest in 5.4 seconds. With the restrictor removed, that time dropped to just 5.0 seconds.

1995: THE M3 LIGHTWEIGHT

It was not long after the E36 M3 had been released in the USA that motor sport enthusiasts began to ask BMW North America for a version of the car that would be competitive

The M3 Lightweight built for the US market was immediately recognizable by its chequered-flag graphics on the bonnet. All pictures of this car were taken by Nick Dimbleby.

The tall rear spoiler was another characteristic of the M3 Lightweight. As this picture shows, there were matching chequered-flag graphics at the rear of the car.

Air bags were a mandatory fitment in the USA by the time of the M3 Lightweight, and so the cars had an appropriate steering wheel – but still with the tricolour Motorsport stitching around the rim.

against Porsche 911s in club-level sports-car races. Clear that the demand was there, the US importers therefore persuaded BMW in Germany to build a special run of lightened cars, which became known as M3 Lightweights. Exactly how many were made is still controversial. Some sources say that there were eighty-five cars, while it appears that BMW promised to build approximately 100. Best guesses are that there were in fact 116 of them although some experts believe that there was as many as 125.

The cars were built at Regensburg but were modified and supplied with additional equipment in the USA. The contract for this work went to PTG Racing (the initials stand for Prototype Technology Group) in Virginia. PTG also prepared two 'cosmetic' prototypes, which were used as press cars when the model was announced in January 1995 before Lightweight production had begun, but they were not actually M3 Lightweights.

As built in Germany in the late summer and autumn of 1995, the Lightweights were 91kg (201lb) lighter than the standard M3 Coupés of the time. They had aluminium door skins, thinner underbody insulation, no underbonnet insulation, lightweight carpets and in the boot there was carpet only on the floor. There was no sunroof and the seats were not available with leather upholstery. Air conditioning was deleted (although it could be added as a dealer option) and there was no radio, although the speakers and wiring remained in place. Even the tool kit was deleted. All cars were Alpine White, and the seats had black cloth upholstery with a red fleck pattern. There was carbon-fibre panelling on the centre console, door sills and facia. The kick plates carried a BMW Motorsport International logo, and there was a similar plaque on the glovebox.

The legend is that BMW selected the most powerful engines from their US-specification stock (there is always some variation between mass-produced engines) for these cars. The speed limiter was then removed from the ECU. A sports suspension of stiffer springs and dampers was specified, and for track use a racing-specification suspension could be ordered through BMW North America. The lower 3.23:1 axle ratio of the US-specification automatic M3s was fitted to aid acceleration. The forged alloy Double-Spoke wheels had the sports combination of 7.5J rims at the front and 8.5J rims at the rear. Standard were a GT-style front spoiler and a GT-style rear wing spoiler.

When the cars were delivered to PTG, the American company added chequered flag decals diagonally across opposite front and rear quarters. They also supplied (but did not fit) a so-called 'trunk kit' of competition accessories. Buyers of the cars were obliged to sign a legal document explaining that fitting these parts would nullify the standard BMW warranty!

The 'trunk kit' (so called because it was supplied in the car's trunk, or boot) consisted of a special sump and longer dipstick tube, a special twin-rotor oil pump, a front strut bar and lower cross-brace, spacer blocks to raise the rear wing spoiler and a unique spring-loaded extendable splitter for the front air dam that could be removed for street use. The later cars were in fact supplied without the trunk kit, but buyers of an M3 Lightweight were able to order the items at no cost.

1998: THE M3 EVO INDIVIDUAL

The end of E36 M3 production for European markets was marked with a limited-edition Coupé known as the Evo Individual, although it is often called the GT2 by enthusiasts and those in the motor trade. There were 200 of these cars, all for Europe, with fifty numbered examples in RHD for the UK. All were painted in Imola Red (BMW code 405),

a colour not available on other M3s, and had upholstery in Imola Red Nappa leather with bolsters and headrests in Anthracite Amaretto suede.

The front spoiler had Class II corner extensions and there was a GT Class II rear spoiler. All indicator lenses had a clear finish. A sports steering wheel with airbag was standard, together with side airbags, electric front seats, an electric sunroof, electric rear side windows and the top Harman/Kardon audio system. The wheels were polished Double-Spoke alloys.

1999: THE M3 ANNIVERSARY EDITION

As far as the Australians were concerned, the M3 Anniversary Edition that appeared in 1999, to commemorate twenty-five years of the M division, was a special treat because it included the only convertible versions of the E36 M3 they were ever offered. There were seventy of these, together with fifty Coupés, and each car had an individually numbered identification plate in sterling silver on the centre console.

The cars were mechanically standard, but they did have a distinctive specification that had been created by BMW Individual, which included special paints and upholstery options. All of them had polished M Double-Spoke wheels, remote locking with an alarm, automatic climate control, a ten-speaker audio system with CD changer, an on-board computer, cruise control, a front armrest and rear headrests. Coupés had an electric sunroof as standard, and the roof of Convertibles was also power-operated. Convertibles also had heated front seats as standard. The SMG gearbox was an extra-cost option, as were electrically adjustable front seats and the top-specification Harman/Kardon audio system. Convertibles could be had with Park Distance Control at extra cost, but bizarrely this was not available for the Coupés.

The paint options differed between Coupés and Convertibles. The closed cars came in Aegean Blue, Cosmos Black, Dakar Yellow, Estoril Blue or Fern Green, and the Convertibles were available in Cosmos Black, Dakar Yellow, Estoril Blue, Fern Green, Imola Red, Techno Violet or Titanium Silver. All the cars had 'extended' Nappa leather as standard, with a choice of Black, Light Grey, Mulberry or Modena Natur, and there was also 'extended' wood trim in Anthracite Birch or (with Modena Natur leather only) Burl Walnut.

THE E36 M3 IN ITS OWN TIME

Autocar & Motor, *9 December 1992*
The self-conscious '90s call for purity of line to replace the bulging bewinged machismo that so distinguished the M3 in the carefree '80s.

Take another look at that gear lever. M3s used to put first, not fifth, out on its own, in classic racing style. No more. It's a small point, especially as BMW says a conventional layout is the more popular, but it is significant.

Anyone who has driven the latest 3 Series will feel at home as immediately as any old M3 driver will feel alienated [...] I struggled to see the difference between this and the 325i Coupé that had been my transport for the previous week [...] where was the thrill, that raw seam of inspiration that, in M3s of yore, captured your heart and mind as soon as you saw the car and didn't let go until you were safely home again?

It may have six cylinders, but the heart and soul of the M3 lives and breathes in this engine as much as ever before... [but] the same cannot be said for the chassis and steering. The old M3's precision, its essence of all that is good in a racing car's chassis distilled into a civilized road machine, has gone.

[This M3] has missed the point. It is not the first car to mistake pace for pleasure and it will surely not be the last [...] But if you expect it to encapsulate the spirit of the true road racer as its forerunner did so well, you are likely to be disappointed. I know I was.

Motor Sport, *January 1993*
Nothing but the badge and its origins in BMW Motorsport really link the new M3 to its predecessor.

The engine has all the hallmarks of BMW breeding, whirring along at low rpm, where there is plentiful torque available, and gradually taking on the note that encourages lazy colleagues to recall the 'turbine smoothness' of a BMW straight six [...] the seductive engine is reason enough to buy.

M3 abilities that set new benchmarks are those enormous brakes and a beautifully absorbent ride.

On dry surfaces there is enormous grip... [but when] surfaces go from dry to damp to wet and back to dry, the M3 is far from convincing [...] the steering fails to relay

either the drop in bite being achieved by the front wheels, or the disquieting speed with which the rears will now want to overtake their forward comrades [...] the new M3 is hard to balance in its new, heavyweight guise.

The new M3 can't match the old when it comes to seeking pleasure on a twisty road... [but] the truth may be that journalists and purists enjoy these original Motorsport devices, but the buying public always want further equipment. Such bulk soon ruins handling pleasure.

[Changing the car's name] would prevent purchasers gaining the false impression that the new M3 is as raunchy a driving machine as the original.

Motor Trend, *March 1993*
Launching from a stop produces instant response; the precision-made screamer starts quickly and easily fills its lungs all the way to the redline, producing power in a continuous, breakneck ascent. The gear ratios are well spaced, smooth in operation, and excellently matched to the engine's torque.

Handling was comparable to the best from Japan and those 'other' European manufacturers of sports cars [...] and you have a car with absolutely magnificent stopping power under any conditions.

With the new M3, BMW once again has proven it remembers well its heritage, understands what the enthusiast wants, and has a knack for turning visions into dazzling reality.

BMW Car, *September 1995*
(The car tested was an Evolution Coupé.)
The party piece of the new M3's chassis has to be those amazing front brakes, imported from the M5.

The engine is a jewel. There's no vibration anywhere in the rev range, but just enough of that urgent yet muted BMW howl has been dialled in to remind the customer of what's below the M-Power cam cover.

Equally impressive is the torque [...] Regardless of the gear, you just squeeze the throttle and go.

If we do have a criticism of the M3 it's that it lacks the raw feel of the original E30 M3. The present model has even been condemned by some as a yuppy car. But we were happy to revel in [its] sheer toe-tingling pleasure.

The racing M3 GT-R was successful in the hands of Johnny Cecotto in the 1993 Warsteiner-ADAC Cup series in Germany.

The E36 M3s were entered for Group N events, and a Group N Coupé is seen here during track testing.

THE E36 M3 IN MOTOR SPORT

In 1993, the FIA replaced the Group A events in which the E30 M3s had been so successful with a new 2-litre category known as the Super Touring class. This new engine-size limitation automatically disqualified the new 3-litre M3 from front-line competition, and in its place BMW fielded race-developed versions of the E36 318i. Nevertheless, the E36 M3 was certainly not absent from the tracks in Europe altogether.

In Germany, the M3 GT-R was developed to compete in the Warsteiner-ADAC GT Cup series. With 325PS and an overall weight of 1,300kg (2,866lb), it proved successful in the hands of Kris Nissen and established BMW driver Johnny Cecotto, who took it to victory in the 1993 series. In Austria, Dieter Quester drove an E36 M3 to the national championship title, and in Holland Peter Kox won the Over-2-litre Touring Car category. There were Group N entries raced by the Warthofer Ladies' Team of Sabine Schmitz and Astrid Grunfelder. In the former Eastern Europe, Vaclav Bervid became a double champion with titles in both Slovakia and the Czech Republic.

M3s also claimed several European hill-climb championships. Xavier Riera took the Spanish title, Francisco Egozcue

In 1992, Italian artist Sandro Chia was invited to create the 13th BMW Art Car from an M3 racer. He is seen here working on the car.

won a European Hill-Climb Championship, and François Doieres took a European Touring Car Hill-Climb title.

BMW of North America began its first ever M3 racing programme in 1995, when it commissioned Tom Milner's Virginia-based Prototype Technology Group (PTG) to oversee its entry into the IMSA GT series. Over the next few years, the M3 dominated the GT classes of sports car racing in the USA. In 1996, racing E36 M3 models took the manufacturers' title in the IMSA (International Motor Sports Association) GTS-2 class in 1996. In 1997, they claimed the manufacturers' title for BMW in the 1997 GTS-3 Sports Car category, when Bill Auberlen also took the drivers' championship with BMW Team PTG. That year, the M3 became one of the few cars ever to win its class at both the 24 Hours of Daytona and the 12 Hours of Sebring. Then in 1998, M3s went on to pull off the same remarkable feat again.

For 1998, the M3s gained BMW the manufacturers' title in the GT3 Sports Car category, with Mark Simo as champion driver. Also in 1998, it was BMW again who won the manufacturers' title in the USRRC (United States Road Racing Championship) GT3 class, while Ross Bentley took the drivers' title. Then 1999 saw the first season of the ALMS (American Le Mans Series), which replaced the IMSA GT Championship. Once again, PTG campaigned M3s on behalf of BMW North America, and this year they came away with the GT class title. But this would be the last racing season for the E36 models; for 2000, BMW North America and PTG would switch to the new E46 cars.

SO YOU WANT TO BUY AN E36 M3?

The E36 M3 shares more components with contemporary mainstream models than any other M3, and has therefore become something of an enthusiast's favourite. That in itself may be a good thing, but it also means that a number of cars will have been run on a shoestring and without the regular expert attention that they need. As these cars get older – and at the time of writing in 2013, even the newest was fourteen years old – more and more things are likely to go wrong with them or be neglected. So what appears to be a bargain at first sight may turn into a money pit very quickly. However, high mileage in itself is not a problem, as long as the car has been regularly and properly serviced.

Rust is not a major problem on the E36, but it does occur. The rear wheel arches are the most likely place to find it,

although certainly not the only one. Check around the jacking rubber points as well. The bonnet edges can rust, and so can the boot lid, around the BMW badges and the boot lock. Inside the boot, remove the carpet and look for corrosion inside the rear panel, behind the number plate and around the lights. The bottom edges of the boot lid can also rust around the drain holes.

Far more common than rust is repair work after accident damage from over-enthusiastic driving. The bonnet gaps should be even, and new bonnet catches may be a sign that they have been replaced after a front-end collision. Untidy seam welds on the inner wings may also show where repairs have been made, and it is a bad sign if the labels applied to the front panel and inner wings are missing: repairers rarely bother to replace them. Loose or poorly-fitting bumpers also suggest 'budget' repair work, as do ill-fitting doors.

Along the flanks, the side mouldings will began to peel away if their retaining clips rust and break off. The seals on the rear side windows and at the bottom of the rear window can degrade, and the door rubbers can split. All these problems may allow water to get into the car, so check for damage inside. The holes under the sill trims can also trap water that eventually leads to rust.

Wheels may have suffered from kerbing damage. Damage to diamond-turned wheels can be particularly expensive, because they cannot be refurbished by the usual methods and replacement is really the only sensible option. Tyres are a good indication of the way a car has been kept, and of the way it has been driven. They are expensive to buy, so beware of cheap replacements, and beware of incorrect sizes. The correct sizes for the car (and not all are the same) will be marked on a sticker beside the catch for the driver's door.

Inside the car, check that all the switches do what they are supposed to do. The powered roof on Convertibles needs to work smoothly and properly, and electric windows in particular can be troublesome. They should operate smoothly and without any hesitation when the button is pressed; if not, either the regulator or the motor may be faulty. The air conditioning is also worth a careful check, because repairs can be expensive. Poor airflow from the system (and from the heater), especially if accompanied by a damp smell, may suggest that the pollen microfilter has become clogged.

On 1995-model and later cars, it is worth ensuring that there are two keys with the car. These cars have an EWS transponder key that 'talks' to the car and has to be paired with it electronically. This pairing can only be done by BMW dealers and specialists, and the local key-cutting establishment cannot do the job.

All these checks are worth carrying out before opening the bonnet, even though the temptation may be otherwise! A visual check of the engine is the first stage, including the usual look at water and oil levels. Remember that an excessively clean engine may have been carefully freshened up to disguise leaks, to which the E36 M3 is unusually prone.

Oil leaks are not uncommon, and the oil pressure valve can leak on high-mileage cars. Valve-cover gaskets leak too, allowing oil to get into the spark plug holes and damage the ignition coils. A smell of burning oil is always a bad sign.

Any temperature gauge that reads above 3/4 is warning of expensive trouble ahead. The plastic radiator tanks can crack around their necks and leak, and radiators will probably begin to leak after 80,000 miles or so. The thermostat housings can also crack. Water pumps are unlikely to last beyond 80,000 miles, and fan clutches fail at about the same time. To check the fan clutch, try turning the fan by hand when the engine is hot (and switched off!); if it spins freely, the clutch has failed. One piece of good news, however, is that head gaskets are not a particular problem, generally lasting at least 100,000 miles and often as long as 150,000 miles.

The VANOS system (and the double-VANOS type on Evolution models) is generally seen as a weakness on these engines. Rattles from the system warn of trouble, although some ticking from the hydraulic tappets is no cause for concern. The most common VANOS problem is leaking solenoid seals, and the solenoids themselves can also seize; gears can wear and fail too but should not in a well-maintained engine.

If the engine is lumpy at idle, a likely cause is failed Lambda sensors. These may burn out after 60,000 miles or so, and if they fail, fuel consumption may increase as well. A squealing noise from the engine bay suggests worn belt tensioners or idler pulleys, and it is important for the belts themselves to be in good condition because they drive the water pump as well as the power steering and the alternator.

It is always worth taking a good look at the exhaust system on an E36 M3. The catalytic converters can rust at both front and rear where they attach to the exhaust pipe, and are very expensive to replace. The rear silencer box is also an expensive item. On Evo models, a flexible section on one of the manifold downpipes can crack. For all these reasons, enthusiast owners often fit aftermarket 'performance' exhaust systems, which may release a little more power but which can also be noisy.

The manual gearbox is generally durable, but check for worn second-gear synchromesh. Play in the gear lever suggests worn linkages. The clutch should last at least 75,000 miles, but on a hard-worked car its life may be shorter, so make sure that it is not slipping. A common fault on higher-mileage cars is clutch drag, caused by a swollen hydraulic pipe.

The SMG gearbox on the Evolution models, on the other hand, has a less robust reputation. If its hydraulic system is low on fluid, the gearbox may jump out of gear and into neutral while the car is on the move, probably accompanied by an error code flashing up on the instrument panel. Clutches can slip here too, and the best way to check is to select the automatic Sport mode when the car is warm, and then drive it hard through the gears, listening for signs of slippage.

The suspension of the M3 is stiff enough for most purposes, and uprating it with harder bushes and the like usually ruins the ride. Steering wander suggests worn suspension arm bushes, and nervousness at motorway speeds points to worn rear trailing-arm bushes and possibly also rear damper top mountings (which will knock when the suspension is bounced). Changing the suspension bushes is not a job for the faint-hearted. Dampers are unlikely to last much beyond 60,000 miles. The cornering should feel very slick: if not, check the anti-roll-bar bushes.

CHAPTER SIX

THE E46 M3, 2000–06

The success of the E36 had certainly set the scene for the M3 models of the future. Its successor, based on the E46 3 Series that was announced in 1997, was one of the most eagerly awaited new cars of its time – and of course BMW played to the gallery on this one.

The 'old' E36 M3s remained available into 1998 – and into 1999 in North America – and of course it was obvious that an M3 derivative of the new E46 would be coming sooner or later. But would it be based on the four-door

saloon or on the forthcoming new coupé? Would there be a Convertible as well? In fact, a study of the E36 M3's production history would have shown that a saloon was most unlikely, as the saloon versions of that model had been withdrawn early – and had actually only been introduced to cover for the temporary absence of a four-door M5 from the BMW line-up.

And so it turned out. BMW announced the coupé version of the E46 range at the Frankfurt Motor Show in autumn

This was the first press picture of the new E46 M3. The car was of course based on the new Coupé body, and this picture shows very well the fatter wheel arches and sporting stance of the high-performance derivative.

The first E46 models to be released were the standard production cars, of which this 318i saloon is typical. The lines were more rounded than on the E36 range, and of course the design had taken into account the eventual needs of the M3 derivatives.

1999, and alongside it they showed what they called a Design Study for the new M3. It was, of course, a coupé – although it did not give away too much about the shape of the eventual production model, being almost deliberately misleading in some respects. Actual deliveries were just a year away, and the first E46 M3s became available in autumn 2000 as 2001-model cars, after a formal launch at the Paris Motor Show.

However, the launch of the new models was actually spread over a period of around five months. Although production of the E46 M3 Coupé may have begun in September 2000, it was initially available only with left-hand drive, and not for North America. Right-hand-drive markets such as the UK had to wait until February for production of their M3s to begin, and so did North America. The final stages of the new-model introduction did not take place until even later, as a left-hand-drive M3 Convertible for Europe entered production in March, followed by right-hand-drive and North American derivatives in April.

Though the tail-light clusters are those of the E46 range, the M3 badge was recognizably the same design that had appeared on the original E30 models.

All this delay was carefully planned, not only to help build customer interest in the new models but also to allow BMW to get production of the mainstream E46 cars running smoothly before they embarked on the special derivatives. And enthusiasts should never forget that the E46 M3 was as much of a headache to the production planners as it was a sales success and image-maker for BMW as a whole.

DEVELOPING THE E46 RANGE

The E46 3 Series range was developed by teams working to Dr Wolfgang Ziebart, BMW's Director of Small Cars. Although design work in the shape of preliminary sketches had probably begun by the end of 1993, BMW claimed that actual product development time had been precisely twenty-four months. The saloon derivatives were made public at the Geneva Motor Show in March 1997. Although the likely requirements of the high-performance M3 derivatives were taken into account from very early on, it is again important to remember that the M3 was not a standalone design but rather a special derivative of a mass-produced car. So a great deal about the E46 M3 was dictated by the requirements of the more mundane models in the range.

One of these requirements was that the E46 should be bigger than the E36 range it replaced. The E36 had certainly been seriously short of rear legroom, and indeed its key rival from Mercedes-Benz, the 190 or W201 range, had been replaced during 1994 by a new W202 (called the C-class) model that delivered much more acceptable cabin space. The BMW design engineers probably intended to improve the cabin space in the E46 anyway, but they could certainly not fail to do so once Mercedes had taken the lead.

Dimensionally then, the E46 was drawn up with an extra 25mm (1in) in its wheelbase, which was achieved mainly by pushing the front wheels nearer to the nose of the car. This in turn set the engine further back to achieve a near-perfect front-to-rear weight balance. In saloon form, the car ended up 38mm (1.5in) longer, 22mm (0.87in) taller and a valuable 41mm (1.6in) wider. Yet, despite these changes, the increase in rear legroom was realistically not all that great.

The new bodyshell was designed to make extensive use of high-strength steel, partly to save weight, partly to improve crash safety and partly to increase body rigidity to improve handling. BMW claimed that the E46 Saloon shell was 60 per cent stiffer and more stable than its predecessor, and that it could absorb two and a half times as much collision energy as the shell from the E30 of ten years earlier. Not only had a great deal of careful design gone into the front and rear crash-deformation zones, but side-impact protection had also figured high on the list of design priorities, and all the doors were strengthened by interlocking internal diagonal bars.

Visually, the E46 brought no real surprises. It looked like a reworked version of the E36, incorporating familiar 1990s BMW family features like the kick-up in the trailing edge of

Behind the trademark twin-kidney grille, the shape was picked up by the air intakes ahead of the cooling fan.

RIGHT: **By this stage, the M3's steering wheel was a multi-function type. On this RHD manual-gearbox car, there are controls for a variety of auxiliary functions. Note the shaped rim that gave better grip, and the M logo at the bottom. The signs of wear on the leather-trimmed rim are fairly typical.**

BELOW: **The electric seat controls included three memory positions. The wear on the leather is again fairly typical, and the appearance can be improved with hide food and other leather treatments.**

the rear window, the L-shaped rear-lamp clusters and the scalloped panel below the headlamps. It also followed the new front-end design pioneered by the E39 5 Series in 1995, with the twin-kidney grilles incorporated into the rounded nose of the bonnet. Many enthusiasts are surprised to hear that the E46 was designed under the direction of Chris Bangle, BMW's American design chief who later took the company in a controversial styling direction with his 'flame-surfacing' style.

Less visibly, there had been some advances in suspension design, even though the basic layout was not very different from that seen on the E36. Most important, perhaps, was the use of aluminium suspension parts to reduce unsprung weight and improve the ride, while wider tracks made their own improvement to stability and handling. ABS was standard, of course, and a suite of braking and traction aids was made available from the beginning.

Passive safety had also exercised the BMW engineers' minds, and the E46 came as standard with a whole collection of improvements to its safety belt and airbag systems. All four main belts had latch tensioners and free limiters, and the front belts were height-adjustable. No fewer than six airbags were standard – two in front, one in each front door, and an ITS head-height bag on each side. At extra cost, Saloon buyers could have an extra pair of bags in the rear doors. All cars also had a sensor in the front passenger seat that prevented the airbag from being deployed if the seat was unoccupied: airbags were too expensive to replace willy-nilly after a collision.

The E46 interior was most attractive, with a dashboard that seemed to flow round to marry up with the front door trims. New 'waterfall' instrument illumination cunningly created a 3D illusion of greater space within the car at night, while traditional dashboard bulbs had been replaced by LEDs that were expected to last the life of the car. The audio system was designed to suit the new dash – and not to fit other cars, so that it was less attractive to thieves. The BMW Check Control system was present, and all cars came with new features called Car Memory and Key Memory. Car Memory programmed such items as the lighting, the air conditioning and the central locking, while Key Memory was activated by the ignition key and automatically adjusted such things as the seat and mirror positions to suit the owner of that key.

Then there were the options. These included AIC rain-sensing wipers, Park Distance Control, xenon headlights, automatic air conditioning, integrated child seats, a heat-reflecting windscreen that reflected infra-red rays, a multi-function steering wheel (with controls for various things other than steering), automatic air recirculation to keep pollutants out of the cabin, a dash monitor screen for the satellite navigation, computer and hi-fi systems, and a less expensive satellite navigation system.

All these features were, of course, made available on the Coupé as well when it arrived in 1999. However, the E46 Coupé was far from being simply a version of the Saloon with fewer doors and a lower roofline. In fact, almost all of its external panels were unique. The windscreen was more steeply raked (by 2 degrees) and there was a longer rear overhang, which was necessary to balance the car visually. There was a special frontal treatment, with a grille, lamps and apron that were all different from the Saloon, the spoiler being deeper with a much larger air intake and circular fog lamps set into its outer ends. The rear apron was different too, being deeper than the Saloon type and incorporating two carefully styled fog guard lamps.

The E46 M3 as most people know it – in Coupé form with the popular Titanium Silver paint of the period. The additional 'power bulge' of the M3's bonnet is clear here.

Inside, the seats were set some 10mm lower in order to compensate for the lower roofline, while the extra length of the trims on the longer doors allowed more stylish sweeping curves in the design. The suspension also was 15mm lower, with 16-inch wheels instead of the 15-inch size standard on the Saloon. Even before the M division got its hands on the car, the E46 Coupé was a most attractive-looking machine.

THE NEW M3 ENGINE

Whatever else goes into the mix to create a new model from BMW's M division, it is always the engine that attracts the most interest. For the engine of the E46 M3, BMW had worked hard to arrive at a specification that could be used for all markets: the need for a very different engine in North America had introduced unwelcome complication and expense into the production of the E36 models. So although there were minor differences to suit regulations in different markets, the new S54 engine was essentially the same for all of them. The biggest variation from its core specification was once again to suit US market emissions regulations: the exhaust catalysts had to be sited slightly closer to the engine block to reduce their warm-up time and so minimize cold-start emissions. It did hit output: the North American engine was very slightly less powerful than the European type.

The magnificent 6-cylinder engine is partially concealed here by the strut brace that was fitted as standard to later cars. This is a RHD UK-market example.

Branding was an important part of the M3's appeal. This is the M division logo on the cam cover of an E46 engine. Visible below it here are the end housings of the Double-VANOS system.

The S54 engine was a further development of the S50 iron-block 'small six' seen in the E36 M3 – and, as things were to turn out, it was the final evolution of this engine. A new and slightly larger swept volume of 3246cc had been achieved by increasing the bore dimension to 87mm from the earlier 86.1mm. The cylinder head was again made of aluminium but this time cast as a single piece in order to save weight; the compression ratio was also raised, to 11.5:1. Finger-type rocker arms reduced both reciprocating mass and friction, and the camshafts were modified. There was now a high-pressure Double-VANOS system, capable of varying the valve timing continuously and of doing so more quickly at high engine revolutions.

The engine-management system was again new, this time known as the MSS 54 type and developed jointly by BMW and Siemens. The six independent throttle bodies used on most engines from the M division were this time electronically operated, and this made possible two M Dynamic Driving Control response modes. Most people referred to this system as a drive-by-wire type. The S54 engine also had a scavenging oil pump to reduce the risk of oil starvation under hard cornering.

Very noticeable to anyone familiar with the old engine was that this one revved higher: it was red-lined at 8,000rpm and delivered its maximum power just 100rpm lower down the rev counter. In European trim, it boasted 343PS – an improvement of nearly 7 per cent on the outgoing S50B32

engine in the E36 M3 – while the North American version of the engine lost an insignificant 5PS from that total. When the new engine was introduced in 2000, BMW were able to boast that it had the highest specific output of any naturally-aspirated engine they had ever made, with the exception of the V12 developed for the McLaren F1 supercar.

Maximum power was less relevant than it might have seemed on paper, of course, because BMW still subscribed to the German manufacturers' agreement and fitted all cars with a limiter that capped the maximum speed at 250km/h (155mph). That was quite fast enough for road use anywhere in the world, but if the limiter was removed (and it could be), the North American cars were supposedly good for 270km/h (168mph), while the European ones were claimed to reach 308km/h (191mph) – a difference which is rather hard to reconcile with a power difference of only 5PS!

Acceleration is, of course, where torque delivery matters, and the S54 engine did not disappoint. Even though it delivered its maximum torque of 365Nm (269lb ft) several hundred revs further round the rev counter than the engine it replaced, there was more than enough of it at lower speeds to retain the M3's characteristic slingshot acceleration.

TRANSMISSION

From the start the E46 M3 was made with a six-speed manual gearbox that was bought in from Getrag. This was essentially similar to the gearbox in the E36 M3 models, though with a small alteration to the second-gear ratio.

BMW had clearly been uneasy about the automatic gearbox option they had offered in the E36 models for North America. Somehow, it seemed wrong for a performance car like the M3 – but the problem was that North American customers were used to two-pedal control and that a very large proportion of M3 customers were in the USA. The SMG electro-hydraulic control system introduced on the E36 models in 1996 had given the best of both worlds, with clutchless changes through a manual gearbox allied to an automatic clutch, although this had never been sold in the USA.

For the E46 models, the solution was to develop the SMG gearbox further so that there would be no need for a conventional automatic gearbox option. This time around, North American customers who wanted two-pedal control would be offered the newly-developed SMG II gearbox, with

ABOVE AND TOP LEFT: **This was the gearshift of a six-speed manual E46 M3, in this case a RHD example. The LED screen was evidence of BMW's increasing use of menu-driven electronics to control many of the M3's more sophisticated functions.**

The SMG transmission could be controlled by Formula-1-style paddle switches on the steering wheel. This one gave upchanges ...

... and this one gave downchanges. The M-branded speedometer of this UK-spec RHD car is visible in the background.

Instead of a conventional gear lever or
automatic selector, the **SMG** cars had this
neat control on the centre console.

The **SMG** cars, of course, had two-pedal control – that
is a footrest on the left of the footwell. Characteristic
of the attention to detail so valued by M3 buyers
is the stitching on the leather trim of the steering
wheel rim, featuring the **M** division's colours.

the latest Drivelogic electronic control software. The same
gearbox would be an option in all the M3's markets around
the world. Though not available from the start of production, it would be introduced in March 2001.

The SMG II gearbox had been developed to give drivers the best of both worlds. Its control software offered
eleven driver-adjustable programs, six in 'sequential' mode
– which meant that the driver selected the gears – and five
in 'automated' mode – which allowed the computer to make
the decisions. On top of that, the SMG II system incorporated the delightfully-named Launch Control function,
which adjusted the automatic shift times to give maximum
acceleration. Drivers had just two pedals, as the clutch was
controlled electronically. Gear changes could be made from
the central selector or by means of the racing-style paddle
shifts on the steering wheel.

The E46 models also had a slightly lower final drive ratio
than their predecessors, which favoured acceleration over
maximum speeds in each gear – but the higher-revving S54
engine ensured that there were no shortcomings in either
department.

DRIVING DYNAMICS

Just as critical as the engine to the overall character of models from BMW's M division are the car's dynamics, and the
engineers in Munich paid special attention to this area of
the E46 M3. So although the car relied on the same basic
suspension, steering and braking layout as the standard E46

models, it had been carefully tuned to deliver a more sporting set of characteristics.

For a start, the M3's structure was stiffened by means of the stronger sub-frame that had been designed to improve the rigidity of the E46 Convertible. The basic layout of MacPherson struts at the front and a multi-link layout at the rear was retained, but there were wider tracks – by 84mm (3.4in) at the front and 46mm (1.8in) at the rear – and larger-diameter anti-roll bars, with a 26mm (1in) bar at the front and a 21.5mm (0.85in) bar at the rear. Special wheel bearings all round took care of the extra stresses to which the M3 would be subjected through enthusiastic driving, and the springs and dampers were all specific to the model, with separate mountings for their top mounting points.

At the front were special 'bat-wing' shaped lower control arms forged from aluminium, with bearings, bushes and cushions all specially developed for the M3. There was a thicker (3mm/0.12in) aluminium thrust plate too. There were special rear-suspension links with steel ball-joints instead of rubber bushes, and the M3 had larger half-shafts and wheel carriers than the standard E46 models. The M-division engineers also decided to settle for 18-inch wheels, with a 19-inch size as an option, in each case with wider rims at the rear than at the front.

The steering was essentially the same as on the standard E46 models, a rack-and-pinion system with speed-variable power assistance. However, there were special joints and a slower overall ratio of 15.4:1 (as compared to the standard E46's 13.7:1). This was designed to give greater 'feel' to the steering. To give optimum stopping power, the BMW M engineers specified ventilated disc brakes on all four wheels, with a diameter of 325mm (12.8in) at the front and an even larger 327mm (12.9-inch) diameter at the rear. On European-specification cars, the discs were of two-piece, or compound, construction, with an aluminium centre-section (sometimes called the 'hat') connected by steel pins to the outer section of the disc. This arrangement was relatively expensive to manufacture but had the big advantage of reducing disc deformation under heavy braking. Nevertheless, the North American specification cars had conventional single-piece discs of the same diameter.

Then, of course, there was a host of electronic traction control aids. These began with a special version of BMW's DSC (Dynamic Stability Control) system that had been developed in conjunction with supplier Alfred Teves GmbH in Frankfurt. Tuned specially to the car, this was able to reduce engine power and/or brake each wheel individually to help maintain traction and control oversteer automatically. However, enthusiastic drivers often object to these automatic interventions (even though they are a major safety benefit), and so the E46 M3 came with an override switch that allowed the DSC system to be switched off completely.

Every E46 M3 was also equipped with the M Differential Lock, an advanced version of the traditional limited-slip differential. Unlike the other traction-control systems on the car, this was activated mechanically rather than electronically. When there was a difference in rotational speed between the two rear wheels, as occurs when one wheel loses grip, pressure was exerted on a viscous silicone fluid. This in turn operated a multi-disc clutch that was able to direct more power to the wheel with the greater traction.

THE FIRST PRODUCTION CARS

The M3 models of the E46 range entered production alongside the more mundane examples of the latest 3 Series at BMW's Regensburg plant near Munich. Both Coupé and Convertible derivatives had a number of quite significant exterior differences from their more conventional E46 brethren.

The front end had a more aggressive appearance, with wider twin-kidney grilles and a deep apron spoiler with large air intakes. The front wings were nearly an inch wider than on the standard cars, and incorporated grille inserts that no doubt deliberately hinted at the grilles that had

Clear in this press picture of a US-specification E46 M3 Convertible are the additional running lights in the front apron, as required by US regulations.

ABOVE: **This was the real thing – a 2000-model M3 Coupé. The air vents behind the front wheels were an instant recognition point for the M division's versions of the E46 series.**

LEFT: **The Convertible would always be the rarest version of the E46 M3. This is a German-specification model dating from 2002.**

Branding again – this time on the air vents in the E46 M3's front wings.

commissioned Michelin to develop a type that featured a compound that would give mild understeer in more extreme circumstances.

There were special features inside the cabin, too. On opening the doors, driver and passengers would first have been struck by the M3 lettering on the sill kick plates. The seats were special M Sport types, and optionally available for the front pair was electric adjustment of the 'wings' on the backrest, to give the most comfortable fit for drivers of different sizes. The steering wheel was a multi-function

Multi-spoke alloy wheels were always part of the package, along with the cross-drilled brake discs just visible here through the spokes.

characterized the big BMW E9 coupés of the late 1960s and early 1970s. The bonnet panel was also unique, with a raised 'power dome' in the centre; less visibly, it saved weight by being made of aluminium.

The M3 also had unique side mouldings that integrated with the side repeater lenses of the direction indicators. All the indicator lenses – front, side and rear – were made of clear plastic, and there were, of course, specially shaped sill panels. Aerodynamic housings for the door mirrors were another special M3 characteristic, and the mirrors could be folded in electrically when the car was parked. Then there were subtly flared rear wheel arches to cover the widened tracks, and a special rear-end treatment too. Four polished stainless-steel exhaust outlets peeped out from under the rear bumper that incorporated an air diffuser. All the aerodynamic changes gave the M3 Coupé a drag coefficient of 0.33.

Inevitably, the M3 also had a set of special wheel designs to help mark it out from lesser E46 models. The standard 18-inch wheels were M Double-Spoke II cast alloys with a Satin Chrome finish. They had 8-inch rims with 225/45ZR18 tyres at the front, and 9-inch rims with 255/40ZR18 tyres at the rear. The optional alternative was available only on European-specification cars in the beginning and consisted of forged 19-inch M Double Spoke II wheels, again with a Satin Chrome finish. These had 8-inch front rims with 225/40ZR19 tyres and 9.5-inch rear rims with 255/35ZR19 tyres. Even the tyres on the E46 M3 were special: BMW

There were optional alloy wheel designs too, always branded with the M logo.

TOP LEFT AND BELOW: **Black upholstery was more or less the default option for the E46 M3, and many owners were content with it. It gave the interior a businesslike appearance totally in keeping with the M3's sporting image.**

The M3 logo on the floor mats was another of those detail touches so much appreciated by M3 buyers.

Lighter upholstery colours created a very different interior ambience from the black. In photographs, they also show the interior details more clearly. In this case, the car's exterior paint was metallic black.

As always, details counted for a lot in the design and presentation of the M3. This was the special kick plate.

This matt silver-grey trim was the default choice for the E46 M3.

type, with button controls for several functions and paddle controls when the SMG II gear system was specified. Then the gauges were branded with the M logo, and the rev counter had a variable redline feature, as first seen on the M5. This was dependent on engine temperature, and was intended to prevent drivers from causing damage by revving a cold engine to its limit. The red section on the dial, which was actually a light shining through the outer rim, moved further round the dial as the engine reached full operating temperature.

The centre console could house a variety of options. In this case, the buyer chose a mobile phone.

In the beginning, there were ten paint options for the new M3. Coupés had six interior colour options, all in Nappa leather, and each of those was available in 'extended' form, with matching leather on the dashboard and centre console – although for unexplained reasons, the 'extended' options were not available in the USA. Convertibles came with the same range of leather options, plus a cloth-and-leather option and an Alcantara-and-leather option, in each case combining grey and black. Both Coupés and Convertibles could be specified with a choice of three different interior trim finishes to complement the upholstery.

The Convertible M3 was inevitably rather heavier than the Coupé when it reached the market in the first quarter of 2001. Mainly, additional body reinforcement to restore the rigidity lost to the absence of a roof panel was to blame, but there was also the small matter of a mass of electrically-controlled hydraulics to raise the canvas roof and of a similar collection of hydraulics to raise rollover bars behind the rear seats in the event of a rollover accident. All this added a massive 180kg (398lb) to the weight of a Coupé in US trim.

For those who wanted it, a removable hardtop was also offered as a rather expensive optional extra for the Convertible. But unless the car was going to spend long periods without being opened to the elements, this was a rather unnecessary luxury. The electro-hydraulic system that raised and lowered the canvas roof could do its job in 22 seconds, and the roof fitted snugly enough for wind noise to be almost non-existent.

There were other compromises with the Convertible, though. The rear seat was narrower than that in the Coupé, and the boot was smaller; in both cases, the space taken up by the convertible top and its mechanism were to blame. However, BMW had done their best: in the boot, it was possible to create more room when the top was erected by folding a panel out of the way.

MINOR CHANGES: THE 2002 AND 2003 CARS

The 2002 model year that began in September 2001 was the first full year for the complete six-model M3 range of Coupés and Convertibles in LHD, RHD and US specifications. With the introduction of the 2002-model cars came a number of small alterations to the specification.

The high-gloss black and Light Maple wood interior trim options had clearly not found many customers, as they now disappeared from the catalogues and were replaced by just one new option, the more subtle Titan Shadow trim. There was a larger 6.5-inch monitor screen for the optional navigation and audio display in the centre stack, and a radio preset function was added to the Car and Key Memory functions, so that drivers did not even have to retune the radio after somebody else had been using the car. Then the optional headlights changed from xenon types to the latest bi-xenon specification; this meant that instead of a halogen high-beam with the xenon dipped-beam light, the high-beam light also used a xenon bulb to give a much brighter light output.

There were also some changes unique to the North American cars for 2002, which gained an in-dash CD player instead of an in-dash cassette tape player. Also standardized were rain-sensing wipers and automatic headlight control.

More incremental changes were made at mid-season, in March 2002, introducing a policy of six-monthly 'refreshers' that would continue throughout the life of the model. There had clearly been some concerns about body rigidity on the early cars, because an 'M Racing' strut brace was added to the front suspension towers as standard. At the same time, the 19-inch alloy wheel option was made available for North America; it seems likely that it was the 19-inch wheels that had been causing shake on earlier cars and that BMW decided to standardize the solution of that strut brace on all cars for the sake of simplicity.

Very little then changed for the 2003-model cars that

became available from September 2002. However, the DSC and ABS control unit did move from the left-hand rear of the engine bay to a new location under the brake fluid reservoir, so leaving a noticeable empty space. BMW also extended their basic Scheduled Maintenance Plan for the cars from its original three years to four years.

There were changes inside the cars too, as the earlier CD-ROM-based navigation system gave way to a DVD-based system that now incorporated an in-dash audio CD player. At the same time a new Brushed Aluminium interior trim option became available.

The six-month 'refresher' that arrived in March 2003 brought two new paint colours, as Mystic Blue metallic replaced Topaz Blue metallic and Silver Grey metallic replaced Steel Grey metallic. The boot handle was also extended, and there was a modified control panel for the automatic climate-control system. A more significant step forward was the introduction of maintenance-free LED adaptive tail lights; these provided two stages of light intensity, the brighter light being automatically selected in the case of very hard or emergency braking in order to give better warning to following drivers. A US press release from February 2003 suggests that US models would get them earlier than European cars and that they would be introduced on these progressively as homologation was approved for individual countries, although in practice it looks as if all M3s had them from March 2003.

THE 2004, 2005 AND 2006 MODELS

In June 2003, just before the start of the 2004 model year, BMW introduced a special derivative of the M3 Coupé called the CSL. Those letters stood for Coupé Sport Leicht (Lightweight Sports Coupé) and they made clear that the car was intended for enthusiastic M3 owners who wanted to use their cars in competitive motor sport. The CSL, which is described in more detail in Chapter 7, was always intended as a limited-production model, was built only from June to December 2003 and was not made available in North America. However, its presence in the M3 line-up meant that the M division saw no need to refresh the standard cars at the start of the 2004 model year in September 2003.

So the only real news for the 2004 model year was that all E46 M3 models would now come with a Bluetooth mobile phone interface and with what was called BMW Assist. M3

Coupés fitted with this were recognizable by a small plastic 'fin' at the rear of the roof, while Convertibles had the fin located on the boot lid.

BMW Assist was essentially a telemetry system that made use of mobile phone networks and the Global Positioning System of satellites. It fed into the satellite navigation system by providing regularly updated traffic information and suggesting alternative routes when necessary. In case of a breakdown or accident, it automatically transmitted the vehicle's location to the emergency or breakdown service to improve response times. It could also be used as a tracking device to locate the vehicle if it was stolen, and (unlike aftermarket tracking devices) was tied into the car's computer systems so that it could not be removed or disabled without rendering the vehicle immobile.

BMW managed without a six-month 'refresher' for the M3 in 2004; clearly sales did not need any additional fillip at this stage. So the next changes came at the start of the 2005 model year in September 2004, when the Laguna Seca Blue and Oxford Green paint options were discontinued. They were not replaced, so reducing the colour choices to just eight.

A further minor change followed in December 2004, when the front suspension of Coupé models was modified to reduce understeer. Of much greater interest to enthusiastic drivers, however, was the availability from that month of an extra-cost optional Competition Package for M3 Coupés, derived from elements of the M3 CSL specification. This was not so much intended for track use as to give a slightly harder edge to the standard cars. As a form of compensation for the absence of CSL models from North American showrooms, BMW introduced it for North America only at first; other markets had to wait nearly a year before it was offered to them. The Competition Package is described in more detail in Chapter 7.

There was then a mid-season change in March 2005, when Phoenix Yellow paint was removed from the options list. It was not replaced, and the paint colour choices for M3s now stood at seven. Clearly, things were beginning to wind down as production of the E46 M3 models approached its end, and as the 2006 model year opened in September 2005 there was another deletion. This time, the cloth-and-leather upholstery option for the Convertible models was discontinued and not replaced.

The E46 M3 Coupé was in many ways a subtle design: the multiple differences from the standard E46 Coupé were not immediately obvious to anybody who took a casual glance, but M3 aficionados always took great pleasure in them.

Nevertheless, this thinning-out of options was largely disguised by the introduction from September 2005 of the Competition Package for European-specification cars. In the UK, as Chapter 7 explains, it was used to create a separate variant of the M3 Coupé that was marketed as the Club Sport or CS model. However, this would be the last fling for the E46 M3. The E46 range was due to end production in the summer of 2006, and with it would go the M3 derivatives. The last E46 M3s were built in August 2006, but M3 enthusiasts would not have to wait as long as usual before there was news about successor models.

ACRONYMS

With the E46 range came a large number of new electronic systems that BMW identified by acronyms. Interestingly, these acronyms were mainly for the English rather than the German names; nevertheless, ABS and VANOS (both acronyms of the German names) were already established and remained unchanged.

ABS	The letters stand for Anti-Blockier System, although they are sometimes explained as meaning Anti-lock Braking System. The system operates through wheel sensors that detect when one wheel is spinning at a different speed from the others, as typically happens if a wheel locks up under braking. Electronics then pulse the brake on that wheel rapidly, to allow it to regain traction. The wheel sensors and electronic circuitry of the ABS system are the foundation on which other traction aids are built.
AGS	The Adaptive Gearbox System adapts the shift points in the automatic gearbox to suit the driver's style.
AIC	Automatic Intermittent Control senses the amount of rain falling on the windscreen and adjusts the wiper speed or delay to suit.
ASC+T	Automatic Stability Control and Traction detects wheelspin through the ABS system and brakes the spinning wheel or wheels until traction is regained.
CBC	Cornering Brake Control uses the ABS sensors to prevent oversteer or a slide if the brakes are applied at extremes of traction, such as during very hard cornering.
CCC	The Controlled Converter Clutch limits torque-converter slip in automatic gearboxes.

DSC III	Dynamic Stability Control (MkIII) measures steering input, yaw angle and transverse acceleration to determine whether a cornering car is likely to drift off the desired trajectory. To keep the car under control, it can reduce engine power and apply brakes to individual wheels.
EWS III	This is the BMW immobilizer system, in its third incarnation on the E46 models.
ICIM	The Individually-Controlled Intake Manifold system varies the effective length of each inlet tract in order to maximize torque. It is operated through the engine control module.
ITS	Inflatable Tubular Structures are head-height airbags located above the windows and under the headlining.
OBD	On-Board Diagnosis is a system that allows an external code reader to be plugged into the engine to 'diagnose' problems by reading stored fault codes.
PDC	Park Distance Control uses radar sensors in the bumpers that trigger an audible warning system to alert the driver that the car is close to obstacles.
SII	The Service Interval Indicator informs the driver of when the next engine oil change is due.
SRS	The Supplementary Restraint System (an industry-standard name) is the front airbags in a car.
TPC	Tyre Pressure Control monitors air pressure in each tyre and can alert the driver to a loss of pressure.
VANOS	VAriable NOckenwelle Steuerung (or Variable Camshaft Control) alters the position of the camshaft and therefore the valve timing to give optimum engine performance at all engine speeds.

COLOURS AND TRIMS FOR E46 M3 MODELS

Paint
There were fourteen different paint colours available for the E46 M3 over the years. Five colours were available from the start of production to the end. Two colours were replaced by variations on the same base colour during production, and two more were withdrawn but not replaced. Two further colours were available on special models only.

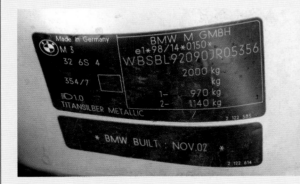

Details of an E46 M3 were carried on these identification stickers attached to the left-hand front suspension tower. The paint names were always given in their German form; this is of course Titanium Silver.

The colours are shown in the table below, together with production dates. The numbers are the BMW paint codes.

Black	Blue	Green	Grey
Jet Black – 668 (09/00 to 08/06)	Laguna Seca Blue – 448 (09/00 to 08/04)	Oxford Green II metallic – 430 (09/00 to 08/04)	Steel Grey metallic – 400 (09/00 to 02/03)
Carbon Black metallic – 416 (09/00 to 08/06)	Topaz Blue metallic – 364 (09/00 to 02/03)		Silver Grey metallic – A08 (03/03 to 08/06)
Black Sapphire metallic – 475 (05/03 to 12/03) *	Mystic Blue metallic – A07 (02/03 to 08/06)		
	Interlagos Blue metallic – A30 (12/04 to 05/06) †		

Red	Silver	White	Yellow
Imola Red II – 405 (09/00 to 08/06)	Titanium Silver metallic – 354 (09/00 to 08/06)	Alpine White III – 300 (09/00 to 8/06)	Phoenix Yellow metallic – 445 (09/00 to 02/05)

* CSL models only
† With Competition Package and for UK-model Club Sport only.

Upholstery – Coupés
Upholstery was in Nappa leather on all models except the M3 CSL. All six colours were available from start to finish of production, but 'extended' Nappa leather was not available in the USA.
   Upholstery on the M3 CSL Coupés was in Anthracite Reflex cloth with Anthracite Amaretta, and had code ADAT.

COLOURS AND TRIMS FOR E46 M3 MODELS *continued*

Colour	Code	Colour	Code
Black	N5SW	Imola Red	N5IM
Black extended	L7SW	Imola Red extended	L7IM
Cinnamon	N5ZM	Kiwi	N5OV
Cinnamon extended	L7ZM	Kiwi extended	L7OV
Grey	N5TT	Laguna Seca Blue	N5LS
Grey extended	L7TT	Laguna Seca Blue extended	L7LS

Upholstery – Convertibles

Upholstery was available in Nappa leather, or in cloth with leather and Alcantara with leather. The leather options were the same as for Coupés, and the 'extended' options were not available in the USA.

The cloth-and-leather option combined Anthracite Impulse cloth with Black Nappa leather and had code N5SW. It was available from the start of production until August 2005.

The Alcantara-and-leather option combined Anthracite M Texture Alcantara with Black Nappa leather, and had code F2AT. It was available throughout the production run.

Interior trim

	Code	Availability
Brushed Aluminum Shadow	737	09/02 to 08/06
Eucalyptus Malt Wood	774	09/00 to 08/06
High-Gloss Black	434	09/00 to 08/01
Light Maple Wood	435	09/00 to 08/01 *
Milled-Effect Aluminum	ZCP	12/04 to 05/06 †
Titan Shadow	771	09/01 to 08/06 **

Several types of interior trim were available, ranging from traditional woods to styles with a metallic appearance.

* Not available in the USA but available in all other markets, including Canada.
** Also available with the Competition Package and on UK-market Club Sport cars.
† Available only with the Competition Package and on UK-market Club Sport cars.

E46 M3 SPECIFICATIONS

Engines:

3.2-litre

Type S54 6-cylinder petrol

3245cc (87mm × 91mm)

Twin overhead camshafts, chain-driven

Double-VANOS (variable valve timing on inlet and exhaust
camshafts)

Four valves per cylinder

Seven-bearing crankshaft

Compression ratio 11.3:1

Bosch MSS 54 engine-management system

Catalytic converters standard

343PS at 7,900rpm

338PS at 7,900rpm (US models)

365Nm (269lb ft) at 4,900rpm

355Nm (262lb ft) at 4,900rpm (US models)

Transmission:

Six-speed Getrag Type D manual gearbox

Ratios 4.23:1, 2.53:1, 1.67:1, 1.23:1, 1.00:1, 0.83:1, reverse
3.75:1

Optional six-speed SMG II clutchless transmission

Ratios as for six-speed Getrag manual gearbox

Axle ratio:

3.62:1

Suspension, steering and brakes:

Front suspension with MacPherson struts, coil springs, Boge
gas dampers and anti-roll bar

Rear suspension with multiple links, coil springs, Boge gas
dampers and anti-roll bar

Rack-and-pinion steering with 15.4:1 ratio and standard
power assistance with variable degree of assistance
dependent on speed; 14.5:1 ratio on M3 CSL, UK-market
M3 CS, and as part of the Competition Package

Ventilated disc brakes all round, 325mm (12.8in) on front
wheels and 328mm (12.9in) on rear wheels; compound
discs on European-specification cars; twin hydraulic
circuits; ABS standard

Dimensions:

Overall length:	4,490mm (176.8in)
Overall width:	1,780mm (70.1in)
Overall height:	Coupé 1,370mm (53.9in)
	Convertible 1,356mm (53.4in)
Wheelbase:	2,725mm (107.3in)
Front track:	1,480mm (58.3in)
Rear track:	1,490mm (58.7in)

Wheels and tyres:

7.5J × 18 five-stud alloy wheels with 225/45 ZR 18 front tyres
and 255/40 ZR 18 rear tyres

Unladen weights:

Coupé	1,542kg (3399.5lb)

PERFORMANCE FIGURES FOR E46 M3 MODELS

Coupé	0–60mph	4.8 sec (*Autocar* test figure)	
	0–62mph	4.8 sec (CSL)	
	0–62mph	5.1 sec	
Convertible	0–62mph	5.5 sec	
	0–60mph	5.1 sec (US-spec car tested by *Car and Driver* magazine)	

All cars had an electronic speed limiter that theoretically limited maximum speed to 250km/h (155mph), although *Autocar*
magazine achieved 157mph. With the limiter removed, European-specification cars were said to be capable of 308km/h
(191.38mph) and North American-specification cars of 270km/h (168mph).

E46 M3 VIN CODES AND SEQUENCES

All E46 M3 models have a seventeen-digit Vehicle Identification Number (VIN). This consists of a ten-digit prefix and a seven-digit serial number. The serial number may consist of six numbers or a combination of letters and numbers.

A theoretical example would be:

WBSBL91011JB76543

which decodes as shown below. Alternatives for each position are shown in the right-hand column.

WBS	BMW Motorsport GmbH, Munich
BL91	LHD Coupé, European specification (For alternatives, *see* lists below)
0	Standard placeholder code on European cars 0 = Manual safety belts (on US cars) 2 = Belts and twin airbags (on US cars)
I	Check digit (1–9, or X)
I	2001 model year 2 = 2002 5 = 2005 3 = 2003 6 = 2006 4 = 2004
JB76543	Serial number

The VIN was stamped into the metal of the bodywork on the opposite side of the engine bay, as well as more visibly at the bottom of the windscreen.

Model codes
These are the alternatives for positions four to seven in the VIN prefix.

BL91	ECE-specification Coupé, LHD	BL96	ECE-specification CSL Coupé, RHD
BL92	ECE-specification Coupé, RHD	BR91	ECE-specification Convertible, LHD
BL93	North American-specification Coupé, LHD	BR92	ECE-specification Convertible, LHD
BL95	ECE-specification CSL Coupé, LHD	BR93	North American-specification Convertible, LHD

PRODUCTION FIGURES FOR E46 M3 MODELS

Overall production totals are as follows:

Coupé	54,750, plus 1,383 lightweight CSL models = 56,133
Convertible	29,633
Grand Total	85,766

Production by calendar year was as follows:

Calendar-year	Build total	Calendar-year	Build total
1999	29	2003	19,271
2000	1,300	2004	13,246
2001	15,294	2005	8,436
2002	23,754	2006	4,436
		(Grand Total)	**85,766**

The breakdown of individual types is as follows:

Model		Production	Total	Type total
ECE Coupé	LHD	2000–06	16,038	
	RHD	2001–06	12,510	28,548
N Am Coupé	LHD	2001–06	26,202	26,202
CSL Coupé	LHD	2003	841	
	RHD	2003	542	1,383
ECE Convertible	LHD	200–06	4,822	
	RHD	2001–06	7,234	12,056
N Am Convertible	LHD	2001–06	17,577	17,577
			(Grand Total)	**85,766**

CHAPTER SEVEN

DRIVING, BUYING AND SPECIAL EDITIONS OF THE E46 M3

The E46 M3 sold strongly without the need for the sales support that limited-edition and special-edition models are designed to provide. Nevertheless, a small number of limited-edition models were made. Germany had a special edition to commemorate thirty years of the M division in 2002, and the UK had a Silverstone edition in 2004 and a Club Sport edition in 2005.

In addition, there were two limited-production 'competition specials' that were not made available to the general public. These were the M3 GTR, built for racing in the USA, and the M3 CSL, intended for European tracks.

THE M3 GTR (2001–02)

The M3 GTR came about when early examples of the new E46 M3 proved unable to keep up with the Porsche 996 GT3 cars entered in the American Le Mans (ALMS) racing series, as is explained later on. It was designed purely for competition success – and did indeed prove successful for a time in the hands of Schnitzer Motorsport – but ALMS homologation regulations for 2001 required that a road-going equivalent of the racing cars had to be made available for sale on at least two continents within 12 months.

BMW prepared a road-going edition, but the 2002 ALMS regulations changed to require a minimum of 100 examples for sale and 1,000 engines as well. BMW decided that this was not viable, withdrew the M3 GTR from the ALMS series and scrapped plans for the road-going cars.

The competition cars were first seen in February 2001 and were controversial right from the start. Their key feature was a 500PS 4.0-litre V8 engine in place of the standard M3's straight-six. Rival teams pointed out that no V8 engine was available in a road-going E46, which made the M3 GTR

more of a prototype than the GT it claimed to be. BMW's plans for a road-going derivative took care of such complaints in the short term.

The road-going M3 GTR was announced in February 2002 with a price tag of 25,000 Euros, and then abruptly cancelled. Mystery and controversy always surround cancelled derivatives of any car, and enthusiasts have estimated that anywhere between five and ten examples were built. However, the reality seems to have been rather more prosaic. According to BMW North America, only three examples of the road-going car were ever made, and only one of those was ever seen in public – at a brief event in the USA that lasted less than an hour. It seems likely that these cars were converted from standard M3s, and that they are therefore included in the build totals for the standard cars.

The road-going edition was planned with a lower-powered version of the racing GTR's engine, no doubt heavily reworked to ensure that it was tractable enough for everyday use. The engine was a dry-sump derivative of the all-alloy M60 90-degree V8 production engine that was known as the P60B40 type, and it had a unique 3997cc swept volume. Power output was limited to 380PS at 7,000rpm with 390Nm (288lb ft) of torque at 4,500rpm, and the engine drove the rear wheels through the standard M3's six-speed Getrag manual gearbox. The M Differential Lock was part of the package.

Although the steering rack, brakes and 19-inch M Double-Spoke II alloy wheels were retained from the standard M3 Coupé, the GTR had wider tracks and uprated springs and dampers. Large sections of the body were made from an ultra-lightweight material known as GFP. The initials stand for the German words, *glasfaserverstärktes Polyester* (carbon-fibre reinforced polyester), and this high-tech material from Intertec-Hess GmbH is otherwise mostly used for protective casings, including boxes and cupboards.

The GFP items on the M3 GTR were the redesigned front and rear aprons, the roof, the large fixed rear spoiler and the smaller rear spoiler lip. The car's bonnet, however, was made of aluminium and was distinguished by a pair of louvred cooling ducts. The bodywork was finished in Titanium Silver metallic from the standard M3 paint options list.

On the inside, weight was saved by deleting the rear seat and by fitting lightweight racing seats with large side bolsters and black cloth (or leather as an option). There was a special Aluminium Cube interior trim, and the plates on the door sills read 'M3 GTR'. The dashboard and instruments were standard M3 types, and the steering wheel was like the standard item but had no switches for an audio system or a cruise control.

All this weight-saving work produced a car that weighed 1,350kg (2976lb), which represented a simply enormous saving over the standard M3 Coupé that weighed 1,542kg (3,399.5lb). So the claimed performance of the road-going car – 0–100km/h (0–62mph) in 4.7 seconds – was hardly surprising. Sadly, the car never did go on sale, but several of the features developed for the road-going version did resurface in the later CSL, in the related Competition Package, and in the Silverstone Edition.

Two of the Schnitzer Motorsport cars also resurfaced a couple of years later in European endurance racing events, driven by Pedro Lamy, Dirk Müller, Jörg Müller and Hans-Joachim Stuck. The first occasion was at the 2003 Nürburgring 24 Hours event. In 2004 and 2005, these two cars came first and second in this event. There were also entries in the Spa-Francorchamps 24 Hours events. Inspired by successes such as these, some privately-owned racing teams also prepared E46 Coupés with the 3997cc V8 engine, and saw some success at Nürburgring events.

THE 30 YEARS OF BMW M EDITION, 2002

BMW's Motorsport division, later renamed BMW M, was established in 1972. In spring 2002, the German market was

Still racing in 2009, this is an M3 GTR. R MARSHALL/WIKIMEDIA

The CSL was really a road-going track car. In this picture, the special front apron with its offset single circular air inlet is clear, as are the 19-inch cross-spoke alloy wheels.

the only one to be treated to a limited edition of thirty M3s to commemorate thirty years of the division's existence.

The car was a mechanically standard E46 M3 Coupé with the SMG II gearbox, three unique colour schemes and a number of items as standard that were otherwise extra-cost options. There were ten examples in each of the three colour schemes, which roughly corresponded to the colours of the M division's logo. The colour schemes were:

- Estoril Blue metallic with extended Nappa leather upholstery in Estoril Blue and Black
- Imola Red II with extended Nappa leather upholstery in Imola Red and Black
- Velvet Blue metallic with extended Nappa leather upholstery in Ink Blue and Black

In each case, there was Anthracite Birch wood trim from the BMW Individual options list. The features drawn from the options list were an electric glass sunroof, bi-

xenon headlights, high-gloss Shadowline trim (from BMW Individual), Park Distance Control, a Harman/Kardon audio system and heated front seats.

THE M3 CSL, 2003

Quite a lot of the work that had gone into creating the planned M3 GTR special edition re-emerged in 2003 when BMW announced the M3 CSL. Available only as a Coupé and only to European specification, the CSL took its initials from the legendary 1971 homologation special based on the big 3.0 CS Coupé. The initials then, as again in 2003, stood for 'Coupé Sport Leicht' (Lightweight Sports Coupé).

Just 1,383 of these very special M3 derivatives were built between June and December 2003, 841 having left-hand drive and the remaining 542 having right-hand drive. These build totals are thought to include nineteen pre-production cars with LHD and ten with RHD, built between Septem-

The CSL engine had a higher state of tune than standard, with 360PS. Clear in this picture of a LHD car is the special air intake system with its carbon-fibre appearance and 'BMW M Power' branding.

ber 2002 and February 2003, although these figures are disputed.

Essential to the concept of the CSL was weight saving, and so several components were made from the lightweight GFP that had been pioneered on the M3 GTR. These included the special front apron (also distinguished by its offset single circular air intake), the front bumper support, the rear apron and the roof panel. The reshaped boot lid was made from SMC (Sheet Moulding Compound), a derivative of GFP that can be heat-moulded, and had an integral spoiler instead of the add-on lip used on standard cars. Fibreglass-reinforced plastic formed the rear bumper supports, and was also 'sandwiched' with thermoplastics and foam to cre-

ate the rear bulkhead and boot floor. Extra-thin glass for the rear window made its own contribution, as did a lightweight exhaust system, made of thinner steel than the standard type.

There was weight saving inside as well, with minimal door trim panels made of GFP and no side airbags, a GFP centre console, and GFP in the construction of the seats, which were broadly similar to those in the M3 GTR. A lot of the sound insulation had also been deleted. All this brought weight down by about 10 per cent from the standard car, and BMW claimed that an M3 CSL weighed 1,385kg (3,053lb) – creditably close to the extraordinarily low weight of the aborted M3 GTR.

To go with the light weight, the CSL also had a special engine tune. Its power unit was a modified version of the M3's standard 3.2-litre S54 straight-six with a direct air intake system that dispensed with the standard airflow mass meter. The new intake system was made largely of the light-weight GRP pioneered on the M3 GTR, and took its air direct from a circular opening in the front apron, through larger manifolding; one noticeable result was that the CSL had more intake roar than the standard M3. Modified cam-shafts and exhaust valves helped to raise maximum power to 360PS at 7,900rpm and torque to 370Nm (273lb ft) at 4,300rpm. In addition, engine responsiveness was improved by intake and exhaust manifolds that were slightly straighter than the standard types.

Oddly perhaps, the only transmission available was the SMG II type, which came with a special Launch Control mode that was able to make the transmission change at the optimum points for maximum acceleration. The Drivelogic unit was also improved over the standard M3 type and was capable of making gearshifts in a claimed 0.08 seconds. The final drive was the standard type, with an M Differential Lock, but the DSC system could be switched to M Track Mode by a button on the steering wheel. This did not switch the system off altogether, but it did raise the threshold at which it would intervene, so allowing for some degree of wheelspin.

The CSL's suspension was very similar to that of the standard M3, but featured a number of detail changes. The front coil springs were shorter by one coil, there were altered spring and damper rates all round, and both front and rear anti-roll bars were thicker, the former having a 30.8mm (1.2in) diameter and the latter one of 22.5mm (0.9in). Then there were special aluminium rear suspension links, with stiffer ball-type bushes. The brakes were borrowed from the E39 M5 and featured compound disc construction with a larger 348mm (13.7in) diameter at the front, together with cross-drilling. A quicker steering rack with a 14.5:1 ratio completed the picture.

The wheels – chosen as much for their appearance as their function – were also lightweight types. Standard were unique cross-spoke 19-inch design with wider-than-standard 8.5-inch front rims and 9.5-inch rears. These came with 235/35ZR19 front tyres and 265/30ZR19 rear tyres. As completed at BMW's Regensburg factory, the cars always had semi-slick Michelin Pilot Sport Cup tyres, which were intended primarily for track use. Buyers who wanted a more road-biased car could order the standard M3's 19-inch M Double-Spoke II wheels, with ordinary road tyres.

Cosmetics were still important, even in a track-focused car like the CSL, and so BMW had made sure that it could not be mistaken for anything else. There was a special 'CSL' insert in place of the standard M3 logo on the intake grilles on each front wing, and the boot lid also carried M3 CSL badging – although this could be deleted at customer request. Silver Grey metallic paint from the standard palette was available, but the CSL could also be ordered in a special colour called Black Sapphire metallic, which would never be available on any other E46 M3.

The passenger cabin had a standard E46 M3 dashboard, but the special front seats had racing-style side bolsters and in place of the rear bench came two individual rear seats; all four seats were upholstered in a combination of Anthracite 'Reflex' cloth and Amaretta (synthetic suede). Alcantara was used for the handbrake grip and the steering-wheel rim. That wheel of course did not have the standard M3's buttons for the audio and cruise control systems but featured just one button – for the DSC's M Track Mode. Both door sills had unique tread plates, and the electric mirror control that normally lived on the driver's side door had been rehoused on the centre console. Interior trim was invariably in Titan Shadow.

There were fewer 'toys' than in the standard M3. The CSL came only with electric windows, central locking, a self-dimming rear-view mirror, and the on-board computer. For extra cost, buyers could have an anti-theft alarm, green-tinted windscreen stripe or climate-comfort windscreen, velour floor mats, bi-xenon headlights with headlight washers (although washers were not fitted to cars for the UK),

GOING ONE BETTER THAN THE CSL

In 2007, German tuning specialist G-Power converted an E46 M3 CSL to run the 5.0-litre S85 V10 engine from the contemporary M5. Tuned to deliver 550PS instead of the 507PS of the standard engine, this car had a claimed maximum speed of 335km/h (208mph). Outwardly, the car was almost unchanged from standard, although it did have G-Power's own 20-inch multi-spoke alloy wheels.

This car was built primarily to demonstrate the German tuner's abilities, and probably remained unique.

Park Distance Control, rain sensor with automatic headlight control, automatic climate control and a variety of audio systems. A 'smoker's package' of ashtray and cigarette lighter was a no-cost option, and the otherwise standard 250km/h (155mph) maximum speed limiter could be removed as well.

THE SILVERSTONE EDITION, 2004

The UK has always been a strong market for BMW's M series cars, and in late 2004 it had a special limited edition M3 called the Silverstone. This was never made available in any other country.

The Silverstone Edition – named after one of the country's famous race tacks – consisted of fifty Coupés. The cars were mechanically standard, with either the standard six-speed manual gearbox or the six-speed SMG II type, but were distinguished by a number of special features and a standard package of otherwise optional equipment.

Paint and interior trim came from the BMW Individual range, and the paint was known as Silverstone II Metallic (code 425). The passenger cabin had Dark Estoril Blue 'extended' Nappa leather, which came with leather covers (though in grey) for the gearshift grip, gearshift boot and the handbrake boot. This was complemented by silver Aluminium Cube trim and black floor mats with leather piping in Dark Estoril Blue to match the seats.

The identification stickers under the bonnet of the Silverstone Edition make quite clear what it is. Note that these cars were prepared under the BMW Individual custom-building programme.

Standard equipment drawn from the options list included 19-inch forged M Double-Spoke II alloy wheels, bi-xenon headlights with washers, electric folding door mirrors and Park Distance Control. Inside the cabin, the Harmon/Kardon audio system was standard, together with satellite navigation incorporating a TV function and Bluetooth connectivity.

It's just another M3 to casual onlookers, but the blueish tint to the silver paintwork gives away that this is the UK-only Silverstone Edition with Silverstone Metallic paint.

ABOVE: **The Silverstone Edition did not have its own special kick plates but was instead identified as a creation of the BMW Individual programme.**

TOP RIGHT, ABOVE AND MIDDLE LEFT: **A striking feature of the Silverstone Edition was the Aluminium Cube trim pioneered on the CSL models.**

The Silverstone Edition came with the top-specification Harman/Kardon audio system.

This striking blue trim was a feature of the Silverstone cars, and looked superb with the blueish-silver exterior paint. As on all M3s, the centre front armrest could be swung up out of the way to give access to the stowage areas in the centre console. Note the all-leather handbrake trim.

The Silverstone had 19-inch M Double-Spoke II wheels. As always, the brake discs were cross-drilled as well as ventilated.

LEFT: **Steering-wheel controls on the Silverstone Edition included one for Bluetooth.**

BELOW: **There was no special exterior badging for the Silverstone Edition; the standard M3 logos were enough.**

ABOVE: **The boot trim of the Silverstone Edition was nevertheless standard.**

Bi-xenon headlights with washers were standard on the Silverstone Edition. The washers popped out from beneath the centre of the light unit when required.

The unmistakeable rear of an E46 M3, with four tailpipes and the sensors for the Park Distance Control embedded in the bumper apron.

Detail again: the bodies of the door mirrors had a particularly pleasing shape.

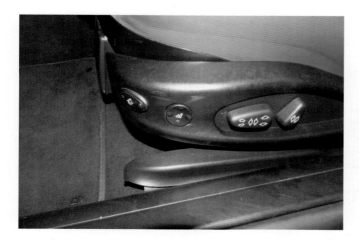

Seat bolster controls can be seen on the base of the passenger seat in this Silverstone Edition.

THE M3 COMPETITION PACKAGE

The M3 Competition Package was introduced in December 2004 for the US market initially, perhaps as compensation for the fact that none of the M3 CSL cars was available for US customers. It subsequently became available in European markets from September 2005; in the UK, it was known as the Club Sport (see below). BMW's own internal designation for it was ZCP, and some enthusiasts choose to call it that.

The Competition Package could be ordered for any new M3 Coupé (but not for Convertibles) and was available with either the manual or SMG II gearboxes. It included no mechanical changes, but consisted of handling enhancements plus one exterior finish option and one interior finish option that were not available on other M3 models.

The suspension had 'a more sporting calibration', as the December 2004 press release put it, although in fact the new spring rates would become standard on all M3s that month, with or without the Competition Package. The new springs in this case were, however, allied to a new wheel-and-tyre package based on 19-inch BBS cross-spoke alloy wheels. Though marketed as forged types, they were in fact spin-cast (flow-formed). These lightweight wheels had 8-inch front rims and 9.5-inch rear rims.

Direct from the M3 CSL came uprated brakes with compound cross-drilled discs and black-painted calipers, and the front discs were enlarged to 345mm (13.6in) from the 325mm (12.8in) of the standard M3. The CSL's M-Track

Mode setting on the DSC was also standardized, with its operating button mounted on the steering wheel. This left no room for the standard wheel-mounted cruise control, radio and telephone controls, which were simply deleted. An Alcantara-trimmed three-spoke steering wheel with matching Alcantara on the handbrake went some way to compensate. Also from the CSL came the quicker steering rack with its 14.5:1 ratio in place of the standard car's 15.4:1.

The unique finishes available only with the Competition Package were Interlagos Blue paintwork and the Aluminium Cube interior trim (by now known as the Special Club Sport type) with a milled effect, that was also used on the 2004 Silverstone Edition in the UK.

The Competition Package went down very well in the USA, where a total of 2,410 cars were sold with it. European-specification cars ordered with the package totalled just 326 – plus a further quantity for the UK-market Club Sport cars.

THE M3 CLUB SPORT, 2005

The M3 Competition Package (see above) was introduced for the US market in December 2004 and became available in other markets from September 2005. In the UK, however, different marketing led to the creation of a model known as the M3 Club Sport or M3 CS, which was essentially an M3 with the Competition Package. A total of 275 examples were built, and in the UK buyers tended to view the Club Sport as a rather more civilized version of the competition-oriented M3 CSL, a car that was almost as sharp in performance and handling terms but was also sufficiently refined for everyday road use. The car cost £2,400 more than a standard £41,115 M3 Coupé in 2005, plus an extra £2,100 if the SMG II gearbox was specified.

Like the Competition Package, the Club Sport was really a collection of enhancements that could be ordered for any new M3. Its primary focus was on handling. To the new spring rates that had become standard on all M3s in December 2004, it added 19-inch BBS alloy wheels with 8-inch rims at the front and 9.5-inch rims at the rear. A more direct steering ratio of 14.5:1 gave quicker turn-in, while the standard DSC system gained what BMW called a 'less intrusive' M-Track Mode that was operated from a button on the steering wheel. Like the CSL, the Club Sport had compound cross-drilled brake discs, with the larger, 345mm (13.6in) size at the front.

THE RACING M3s

There was no place for the M3 in the European Touring Car Championship (which became the World Touring Car Championship in 2005) during the production life of the E46 models. Engine sizes were limited to 2.0 litres, and so BMW campaigned the only car it could, which was the 320i version of the E46. The absence of the M3 from front-line motor sport must have been keenly felt in Garching; it was certainly noted by many enthusiasts for the M brand, even if not all of them understood the reasons for it.

Factory-backed M3s did eventually return to European motor sport, and with hindsight the campaigns with the 320i cars in the first decade of the twenty-first century can be seen as a prelude to the main event. Schnitzer Motorsport ran BMW Team Germany, with Dirk Müller and Jörg Müller as their drivers. Former BMW M3 driver Roberto Ravaglia ran two cars for BMW Team Italy/Spain, with Alessandro Zanardi and Antonio Garcia as drivers. In 2005, BMW Team UK (run by RBM) took their 320i cars to the WTCC manufacturers' title, while driver Andy Priaulx took the drivers' title.

Yet the emphasis on motor sport in so many of the E46 limited editions was not entirely hollow. Although Europe did not see the M3s racing, US racegoers were treated to the sight of E46 M3s in the GT class of ALMS (American Le Mans Series) events during 2000. The cars were prepared by Prototype Technology Group, who had been BMW North America's competition partners since 1995, and were known as M3 GTR types. Unfortunately, their first season was not at all encouraging. The M3 GTR won just one event in the season, which was dominated by the Porsche 911 GT3s.

BMW reasoned that the Porsches were working with a huge advantage. The ALMS rules demanded that both the M3s and the 911s were obliged to use the same size of air intake restrictor plate, but the Porsches had 3.6-litre engines compared with the 3.2 litres of the BMWs. The BMW engine could not be enlarged because of its bore spacing, so BMW decided to do something radical.

Although the first ALMS race of the 2001 season was contested once again by the racing M3 GTRs, a heavily revised race car was rolled out for the second and subsequent events. BMW had thrown out the 6-cylinder engine and in its place had fitted a 4.0-litre V8 developed by the M division specially for the job. Most important was that the engine developed much more bottom-end torque with the obligatory air restrictor in place, as well as more power than the Porsche engines.

Car and Driver magazine summed the car up like this in its March 2003 issue:

> *A six-speed non-synchro gearbox transmits power though a limited-slip rear differential to 11.4-inch-wide Yokohama racing slicks. The V8 M3 uses the same basic chassis as the six. As the rules require, it's based on the stock M3 body shell. But by the time BMW has added safety-cage bars, new suspension bits, carbon-fiber bodywork, front and rear wings, and a data-acquisition system, the GTR is far closer to a purpose-built race car than a street car.*

Two teams campaigned the V8-powered GTR in the 2001 ALMS events, PTG and Bell Motorsports, who had also run earlier M3s in the US series. This time, the M3 had it right: the V8 GTRs claimed that year's manufacturer trophy and team trophy, and Jörg Müller won the drivers' title as well. Porsche were among the rivals who complained that the new GTR was not based on a road-going car, because no V8-engined M3 was available through the showrooms. However, BMW announced plans to produce the required number of such cars.

Then for the 2002 season, the ALMS regulations changed, to require a much larger number of road-going cars for homologation purposes. BMW looked at their options, decided it would be far too costly to comply with the new rules, and cancelled both the planned M3 GTR road car and further competition with the V8-engined E46 in the ALMS events.

Nevertheless, the 6-cylinder cars kept on racing; Alega Motorsport ran an E46 M3 as a private entry in the 2002 series, finishing seventh. Then in 2004, driver Bill Auberlen claimed top honours in the Rolex GT series, when BMW also went home with the team and manufacturer awards.

What nobody outside the BMW factory knew at that stage was that a V8-engined M3 production car was just a few years away.

THE E46 M3 IN ITS OWN TIME

Car and Driver, January 2002
(The car tested was a Convertible.)

The M3 convertible has the combination of effortless energy, secure grip, and linear controls that make any driver feel like [world champion racing driver] Michael Schumacher – and want to emulate him. [It is] by far the quickest droptop on the market with an adult-feasible rear seat. Turn off the traction control, drop the clutch at 4,500 rpm, and you rocket to 60mph in 5.1 seconds. A mere 7.4 seconds later, you'll hit triple digits.

At top speed, on an admittedly uneven road, the M3 cabrio did want both hands on the wheel. But in most other circumstances, it inspires immense confidence. We found ourselves hurling the M3 into corners ever faster, knowing the car was so well-planted on its big Michelin Pilot Sport tires that we would simply track through as if on a tether. Even in fast corners, midcourse corrections are always an option because there's invariably sufficient bite to tighten your line.

Dropping the top is so painless, we often did it for five-minute trips… This top is fully lined and impressively tight. Even during an extended 90-plus-mph cruise – people sure drive rapidly in central California – air leaks and wind roar were so low that we almost forgot we were driving a convertible.

Evo, June 2005
(The car tested was a UK-market M3 CS.)

The CS is essentially an M3 that's borrowed a few tasty bits from its exotic, expensive and now out-of-production CSL sibling… The good news is that the CS has a sharpness and accuracy that the [standard] M3 never quite attains. You'll notice the new steering rack first, with its meatier weighting and more immediate response. Then you'll realize that the ride seems flatter, less disturbed by sharp lumps and bumps passing beneath the wheels. Up the pace and this firm but pliant set-up just gets better and the M3's trademark pogo-ing motion never materialises.

On the down side:

[The] straight-six has too much power for the brakes to rein-in, despite bigger discs. They're overwhelmed by the engine's venom and quickly protest when used hard on the road, with expensive-sounding groans and a soft pedal. Even snicking down through the slightly long-winded manual 'box to help deceleratiom … does little to halt the brakes' decline. Fortunately the CS is so entertaining through the turns that you're happy to drive around the weak brakes and instead revel in one of the most throttle-adjustable chassis in the world.

Overall:

[The] CS has tangible gains in feel and agility and quickly gives you confidence to use all of its potential. The CSL was always a great car with a crazy price-tag. The CS is just a great car, and if you're buying an M3 you'd be crazy not to pay out £2,400 for the added bite, polish and aesthetic attitude that it brings.

SO YOU WANT TO BUY AN E46 M3?

At the time of writing in 2013, the typical mainstream E46 M3 could be bought in the UK for around 15 per cent of its original purchase price. While that made it something of a bargain, it also helped to highlight two points: the first was that the car would still cost as much to run and to maintain as it always had, so that low initial cost was potentially misleading; the second was that many buyers would not realize this until it was too late, and would end up skimping on maintenance in order to keep the car running. So really good, well-maintained cars were likely to become rarer with the passage of time.

As with any M3, buyers need to know as much as possible about the history of a potential purchase. This goes far beyond the regular HPI checks and the like to make sure that the car really does belong to the seller. So a thorough check of documents recording its servicing history is essential – and it is not uncommon to find some faked documents among them, covering up for missed servicing.

Ideally, the paperwork with any car should contain evidence that the original running-in service was carried out at 1,200 miles; this service included an oil change, which experts say was essential for the long-term durability of the engine. Pre-2003 cars were recalled for a check of the engine con-rod bearings, and there should be evidence in the paperwork that this was carried out. A service history with established specialists should be just as reassuring as a service history with a BMW main dealer, but paperwork from an all-makes village garage or rundown backstreet outfit should ring alarm bells.

The first visual check should be of the bodywork, both for accident damage and for corrosion. The front wheel arches are less prone to rust than those on standard E46 3 Series models, mainly because they do not have the same rubber seal on the arch liner to attract mud and retain water. Nevertheless, the rear wheel arches can rust at the point where they meet the rear bumper. Corrosion can also attack the metal around the rear window.

Particularly worth checking is the condition of the door mirror bodies, and whether the associated electrics all work correctly, as replacement mirrors are expensive. On cars fitted with the bi-xenon headlights (introduced in September 2001), it is advisable to check that everything works as it should. The lights' self-levelling system can fail, although the cause is usually nothing more than a defunct relay.

A wise next stage is to look at the tyres. These are expensive, so owners often try to save money here. Non-matching tyres are the usual giveaway, while worn tyres will be very obvious.

Most buyers want to head straight for the engine next. The good news is that it is a strong and reliable power unit. Some of the early cars suffered crank bearing failures at around 30,000 miles, but all of them were (or should have been) dealt with by now. BMW arranged for repairs under warranty, and in some cases replaced the whole engine. There may be evidence of this in the car's paperwork.

Although the double-VANOS variable valve-timing system is more robust on these engines than on their E36 predecessors, it is prone to one problem. This occurs at around 70,000 miles, when the bolts can work loose. Catastrophic engine failure is the result, so it is advisable to make sure the appropriate checking and remedial work have been done.

Less frightening problems are associated with the coil packs and the alternator. Both can fail, but replacement is well within the capabilities of most home mechanics.

There are no special problems with the standard six-speed gearbox, but the SMG II type is not for everybody. A short test-drive might not be enough to allow a buyer to form an opinion, so it is always best to talk to people with experience of the type and, if possible, to gain driving experience with one in less pressurized circumstances than the test drive typically affords.

The SMG on the E36 cars did not earn itself a good reputation, but the E46's SMG II addressed those early problems. All gears should engage properly, in all gearbox modes and at all speeds. Full-throttle work should show the gearbox at its best; lifting off the accelerator at changes may reduce jerkiness and so mask problems. Failure of the hydraulic pump will cause the gearbox to drop into neutral, but so will a relay that is just about to fail. A replacement pump is very expensive; a replacement relay is cheap, and so is the associated labour cost.

All clutches wear if the car has been driven hard, but SMG-equipped cars that have spent a lot of time in town traffic may wear clutches more quickly than ordinary manual

SO YOU WANT TO BUY AN E46 M3? *continued*

M3s. Judder from the clutch as it takes up the drive in the lower gears is a warning that replacement is needed. Worth knowing is that BMW offered an SMG software update that helped reduce clutch judder, and that a conscientious owner will have taken advantage of this.

One characteristic of the E46 M3 that often causes concern is a grinding noise from the differential, typically in tight turns at low speeds. This is simply a characteristic of the model, but it can be alleviated by changing the oil for the later recommended type (made by Castrol), which has special additives.

If the suspension feels less than taut on the road, a likely cause is worn front ball joints, which can be replaced easily. The bushes on the front wishbones and the rear trailing arms are unlikely to last longer than 60,000 miles. Rear coil springs can actually break, but in any case will need to be replaced along with their dampers by around 80,000 miles.

Inevitably, all kinds of aftermarket suspension and brake upgrades have been available for the E46 M3. Kits from the acknowledged BMW aftermarket specialists can usually be relied upon from an engineering point of view, although they may make the ride unacceptably hard. However, cheaper kits may ruin the whole balance of the car, and are probably best avoided. Brake upgrades have often been made so that a car will perform better at track day events, and are likely to be a clue that the car has been used hard.

Opening the doors may reveal loose rubber seals. This is a common problem that is easy to fix, and is caused by poor-quality fixing glue. Sticky door locks suggest that regular greasing (about once every six months) has not been carried out. It is also advisable to check the self-dimming rear view mirror, as the fluid inside the mirror body that effects the darkening of the glass can sometimes leak.

On Convertibles, the folding roof should work smoothly and quickly, and should fit snugly. Slow operation may indicate that regular greasing of the linkages has not been carried out, but a poor fit will indicate bigger problems, which might include cheaply-repaired accident damage.

One problem that particularly afflicted the E46 M3 was cracking of the rear subframe. BMW's policy was to put this right free of charge on cars under ten years old, and in some cases the main-dealer approved solution was to reinforce the subframe by injecting it with a foam filler. If the problem was not caught in time, flexing at the rear end could also cause the boot floor to crack, and in some cars BMW replaced this as well. However, cracks in the boot floor on a car now should ring alarm bells; rectification is a very expensive task, and only the very last E46 M3s are now likely to qualify for BMW's goodwill replacement assistance.

CHAPTER EIGHT

THE E90-SERIES M3s, 2007–13

Ever since the original E21 3 Series models, two-door, four-door and estate models within the range had shared a common project code. This had worked well for the second-generation E30 models, and tolerably well for the third-generation E36. However, by the time of the fourth-generation E46, the number of variants was beginning to cause difficulties.

So for the next generation of 3 Series cars, engineering development chief Burkhard Goeschel decided to subdivide the project into four separate but closely linked elements. As a result, there were four different codes for the different models. The saloons were developed as E90 models and the estates as E91 types, while the coupés became E92s and the convertibles became E93s. Most obviously, this allowed each core type within the planned overall range to proceed at its own pace, so that delays with one would not automatically impact on the others. It was a more efficient way of working that must have reduced stress within the project teams.

Even so, the new E90-series cars did not all appear together. (The term E90-series is used here as a generic description for the whole range; enthusiasts also call them the E9x-series cars.) Their launches were staggered to make production changeovers easier, and to suit the marketing requirement of building anticipation among BMW's customers. So, although the E90 and E91 four-door models were first seen in March 2005, the E92 and E93 two-door types were introduced a year later – and the first M3s were not available for another year after that.

So, as usual, BMW played a waiting game with its customers. But the company was a past master at manipulating anticipation and expectations, and it raised the level of interest with a carefully-timed M3 concept car, revealed at the Geneva Motor Show that opened on 6 March 2007. The company was simply toying with those who were eagerly awaiting the new M3. The real thing appeared at the Frankfurt Motor Show that opened on 13 September – and it was not very different from the concept car. Meanwhile, the media had already driven examples of the new model at a ride-and-drive event in Malaga, Spain during July.

The 2007 M3 concept car was keenly awaited, and was, of course, based on the E92 Coupé. Quad tailpipes, wing vents, sculpted sills and multi-spoke alloy wheels were among the customer expectations that BMW satisfied.

Another new shape of tail light... but the M3 logo was too precious to change.

THE MAINSTREAM E90-SERIES

The eventual requirements of the M3 were taken into account during the early design stages of the E90-series cars, and it was always understood that the M division could make requests for localized reinforcements at the design stage so that the car would be more readily adaptable to its high-performance role. Other areas could be designed around the M requirements too: so, for example, the front suspension was designed to allow for the large-diameter high-performance brake discs that the eventual M3 variant would need. Although the overall layout of the suspension was not startlingly new, BMW took special care from the beginning to reduce weight. So the MacPherson struts used at the front end were made of aluminium, and the components of the five-link rear suspension were made from high-strength steel, which allowed their size to be reduced.

The variety of engine and transmission combinations for the E90-series was, as always, immense, but more important for the M3 story is the design, which was carried out once again under the leadership of Chris Bangle. Although the shapes of the E90-series models were necessarily restrained by the need to appeal to a fairly conservative group of customers, some elements of the sharp-edged lines that were the essence of Bangle's controversial 'flame surfacing' did creep in. The new 3 Series models were much less rounded than their E46 predecessors, with sharp edges in the shapes of the bumpers and side sills, and particularly in the full-length crease that ran along each side of the cars, passing through the door handles. The rear end too was not far removed from what the Americans derisively called the 'Bangle butt' of 2001's big E65 7 Series saloons.

Subdividing the development of the four E90-series models allowed the two-door models to have quite different proportions from the four-doors. Although there were clear family resemblances in details such as that long body-side crease, the Coupés and Convertibles had many special features of their own. Their front ends in particular were quite different, with more rounded grilles, narrower headlamps and a different design of bumper. The bonnet was actually longer than the Saloon type, and the roofline, of course, was lower, while the side skirts were again special. At the rear, the lamp units were wider and the bumper different again. Most of the wheel designs chosen for the two-door cars were also different from those for the four-doors.

Nevertheless, the passenger cabins of the two groups of cars did share common elements, and the dashboard, centre

Cupholders were a standard feature, although their presence was driven largely by US market requirements.

console and front seats were all the same. Rear seats were different, however, as the two-doors had two individual rear seats separated by a console tray, while the four-doors had a bench seat for three passengers. Trim details differed as well, and the two-doors had chromed handles, vents and bezels where the four-doors had aluminium items.

Perhaps the most interesting development was reserved for the Convertibles, which had a folding aluminium hard-top instead of a traditional fabric top on a metal frame. The three-piece top was operated by an electro-hydraulic mechanism and disappeared beneath a metal tonneau cover when not in use, and it could be operated from buttons on the key fob. When the Convertibles were announced in 2007, the only other cars to have such a system were both two-seaters (the Mercedes-Benz SLK and the Mazda MX-5), so the new BMW was a pioneer of such systems for a four-seater car. As was to be expected, the Convertibles also had electrically activated rollover hoops behind the rear seats.

THE NEW M3 POWER TRAIN

There was no more development life left in the old S54 straight-six engine from the M division. BMW had acknowledged as much when it had turned to a special 4.0-litre V8 engine for the E46-based ALMS racers in 2001. So it should not have been an enormous surprise to BMW watchers that the E90-series models were announced with a completely new engine, whose aluminium alloy block was cast in BMW's Formula I foundry at Landshut.

Those abortive ALMS racers had given a clue to the way BMW were thinking, of course, and the new engine that appeared in 2007 was a 4.0-litre 90-degree V8. It was not, however, the same engine that had been created for the ALMS cars. Instead, the new S65B40 from BMW's M division was a close relative of the S85B50 5.0-litre V10 that had been introduced for the M5 models in 2005. That engine had won four International Engine of the Year awards in 2005 and would go on to win many more over the next few years.

It was perfectly logical for the M division's two new engines to share common design features and components, and the basic idea behind the V8 was of a V10 with two of its cylinders lopped off. It shared the V10's 92mm bore and 75.2mm stroke dimensions, its 12.0:1 compression ratio and its Double-VANOS variable-valve-timing system. It was also controlled by a derivative of the Siemens ECU that had been developed for the V10, known as the MSS 60 type. BMW boasted that this was the most advanced engine management computer available in any car at the time; capable of

more than 200 million calculations per second, it was eight times as powerful as the ECU of the old S54 engine. Each cylinder had its own individual throttle butterfly to give a fast and precise response. One result of the close relationship with the V10 was that the V8 ended up with an unusual firing order: 1-5-4-8-7-2-6-3 rather than the more typical 1-5-4-8-6-3-7-2. Another was that it was a much higher-revving engine than the 6-cylinder it replaced.

However, where the larger engine had a dry-sump lubrication system, the V8 had a lighter system with a pair of wet sumps, each one served by its own oil pump. Weight-saving, as always in this stage of BMW's history, had been a high priority during the design stages, and the V8 entered production weighing 15kg (33lb) less than its straight-six predecessor. It also met the forthcoming Euro V and CARB (California Air Resources Board) exhaust emissions regulations, while being shorter than the old engine and developing considerably more power and torque. The new figures were 420PS at 8,300rpm and 400Nm (295lb ft) at 3,900rpm, which compared very favourably with the 360PS and 370Nm (273lb ft) of the most powerful S54 engines in the E46 M3 CSL.

The M3's heart: with the E90-series cars came a V8 engine in place of the straight-six used in their E36 and E46 predecessors.

The engine ancillaries incorporated new technology too, and the alternator automatically declutched itself from the engine during acceleration to reduce power drain. Although there were safety overrides to prevent a car ending up with a flat battery, the alternator generally charged the battery only during braking and deceleration. BMW gave this system a name, in line with company marketing policy. They called it Brake Energy Regeneration.

The new V8 was installed as far back as possible to give optimum weight distribution, and only one of its four pairs of cylinders sat ahead of the front axle line. It was arranged to drive the rear wheels through a twin-disc clutch and six-speed manual gearbox, and this was the only option when the first M3s were made available in 2007, although the M division did have something new up its sleeve for later. The rear end came as standard with the latest Variable M limited-slip differential.

THE FIRST PRODUCTION CARS

The new E90-series M3s were introduced in three stages. First came the E92 Coupé, the core model of the range, which was introduced in September 2007. Next came the E90 Saloon, in March 2008, and last of all came the E93 Convertible, in May 2008. Each of the three models had been extensively re-engineered from its mainstream parent to deliver the driving experience that the M division knew its customers wanted. The Convertible came with the folding metal roof that had now replaced the fabric roof structures of earlier BMW soft-top models.

The suspension had been further developed for lighter weight, with forged aluminium track control arms at the front and an all-aluminium version of the five-link rear system. Standard on Coupés was an Electronic Damper Control system with three settings that could be dialled in from the dashboard, and the other models could have this as an option. The brakes all had new 'compound' discs, with steel top-hat centre sections allied to lightweight aluminium outers that were both ventilated and cross-drilled (a configuration that had been previewed on the CSL variants of the previous E46 generation M3). The standard wheels were 18-inch alloys with wide rims that increased the front and rear track dimensions, and there was a 19-inch option. The steering was sharper than on the mainstream models, and all versions of the M3 came with special Michelin Pilot Sport tyres, developed for the M3 to BMW's own specification.

The front end of an E92 Coupé again shows the detailing that M3 buyers demanded. There is a specially shaped front apron (although this one with its carbon-fibre-look sections was part of the Competition Package), the bonnet boasts a 'power bulge' and the mirrors have an individual shape.

Once again, the E90-series cars had a distinctive rear apron (with Park Distance Control), this time incorporating a diffuser and four tailpipes.

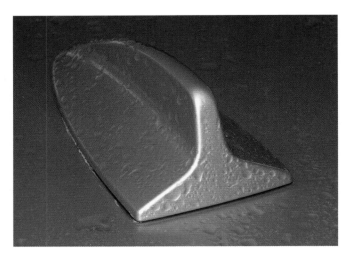

Never particularly attractive was the roof-mounted 'fin' aerial for the satellite navigation system. It remained unchanged on the E90-series cars.

All this was wrapped up in a typically eye-catching collection of changes to the body. All three models came with flared wheel arches to cover the widened tracks, with larger air intake scoops in the front apron and with air vents (many enthusiasts call them 'gills') in the front wings. The bonnet was made of lightweight aluminium and now incorporated a 'power dome' in its centre with an air intake on either side, and the rear panel incorporated a diffuser, which differed between two-door and Saloon models. There were special outer sill panels, a discreet lip spoiler on the boot lid and the M division's trademark four exhaust tailpipes. On Coupés only, the roof panel was made of lightweight carbon fibre, just as it had been on the E46 M3 CSL special edition cars. Saloons and Convertibles shared the Coupé's front-end styling and narrower headlights, which were bi-xenon types as standard with corona rings for use as daytime running lights.

Wing vents had gone down well with customers on the E46 M3, and the idea was retained for the E90-series cars.

The least common and heaviest version of the E90-series M3 was the Convertible, which had a powered metal folding roof.

Multi-spoke alloy wheels were standard as usual: these are the 19-inch option.

Bonnet air grilles were another distinctive
feature of the E90-series M3 derivatives.

The standard tail spoiler was a small lip
attached to the standard boot lid.

As always, there was special seating for the
M3 derivatives of the 3-Series range. This is
the front seat of a RHD saloon; just visible
is the M logo on the head restraint.

All the E90-series cars had special **M3**-branded kick plates... but on Saloons
the rear door opening made do with unbranded plates.

The use of menu-driven controls for the less commonly
used functions enabled **BMW** to clean up the E90-
series dashboard and centre stack considerably.

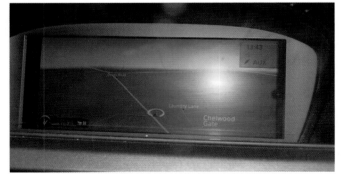

The E90 Saloon in its M3 form made a
really practical car as well as an exhilarating
one. These are the rear seats.

Moving the display screen up alongside the
instrument panel not only made it more readily
visible to the driver but also allowed **BMW**
to reduce clutter on the centre stack.

Less visibly, the front and rear bumpers were carried on lightweight long-fibre thermoplastic mountings. US-market models had additional amber side marker lamps in the outer ends of the front apron.

The special interior features started with M Design dual round instrument dials, which included a 200mph speedometer and a rev counter with graduated amber and red sections to discourage use of maximum revs until the engine oil had reached working temperature. A Control Display could be fitted in the dash centre at extra cost. Coupés had two individual rear seats with a through-loading facility that could be complemented by an optional ski bag. Upholstery was in cloth and leather as standard, but there was an all-leather option in four colours. Regardless of the main upholstery colour, the upper side of the centre console was

The cars came with their own dedicated handbook; owners would not have appreciated a few pages tacked onto the end of a standard E90 Saloon book.

Special touches remained part of the M3 DNA. This is an optional carbon-look mirror body.

upholstered in black leather. When leather upholstery was specified for Convertible models, it had been specially treated so that it reflected sunlight; this so-called SunReflective Technology prevented the leather from becoming uncomfortably hot if the car was left with the roof open in the sun.

There was an impressive array of equipment available for the new M3s. The iDrive system was standard, and included an M Drive menu level, which could be supplemented at extra cost by an M Drive button on the steering wheel. This was programmable, and in effect was a one-touch memory button for the car's drive systems: accelerator response, suspension stiffness and DSC stability control intervention could all be configured to suit the driver's wishes and preset for instant retrieval. This was useful after another driver had been using the car, but it also enabled the driver to transform the car from comfortable town cruiser to hard-edged track-optimized performer in an instant. The M Drive presets could also be extended to alter the apparent weight of the Servotronic steering, at extra cost.

However, the standard options list was only the beginning of the E90-series M3 story. BMW's marketing teams had noted over the years how M3 customers seemed to take a special enjoyment from the process of individualizing their cars with choices from that list. So for the E90-series cars, there was a vast increase in the options through the

The four-door M3 remained available too, this time with E90 identification. This is a UK-market RHD car.

BMW Individual custom-finishing scheme. To a relatively small number of standard paint options (eight colours, four of them new M Metallic types) were added around fifty others, all of which cost extra – and there were three groups of Individual paints, each one more costly than the last. The upholstery and interior trim options were also expanded through the BMW Individual scheme.

Other options included the BMW Individual High-End audio system, satellite navigation, an internet portal, BMW Assist telematics and BMW TeleServices for wireless servicing diagnostics. Buyers could choose to have four horizontal enhancement strips running across the dashboard, and they could choose the Extended Leather option, which brought upholstery to the lower section of the instrument panel, the glove compartment cover and the side panels of the centre console.

Performance of all three M3 derivatives was similar, although the extra 200kg (441lb) weight of the Convertible inevitably made it the slowest. In line with the gentlemen's agreement among German car manufacturers, all M3s were speed-limited electronically to 250km/h (155mph), and this inevitably threw the buyer focus onto acceleration. BMW claimed that an M3 Coupé could reach 100km/h (62mph) from rest in 4.8 seconds, while the heavier

Convertible took 5.3 seconds. In all cases, the new model was blisteringly fast.

THE DCT TRANSMISSION (2008)

As already explained, the M3 was introduced with a six-speed manual gearbox as the only transmission option. There were many buyers who expected a version of the SMG gearbox to become available for those who preferred two-pedal control, but the M division was in fact working on something even better.

That 'something even better' was a dual-clutch transmission with electronic control. Dual-clutch transmissions had been brought to market in 2003 by Volkswagen, who had worked with Borg Warner to develop a system for the Golf. The system worked by using concentric clutches, which acted on alternate gears in the transmission; their main advance was that they allowed lightning-fast gear changes with no interruption of the torque flow from the engine. With an electronic control system, the dual-clutch transmission could be used as a fully automatic gearbox while giving manual override control to a degree that was simply not possible in conventional automatics with a torque converter.

ABOVE, TOP AND MIDDLE RIGHT: **Though a six-speed gearbox was available for the E90-series cars, it was less popular overall than the new DCT transmission. Note here the rotary control for the functions displayed on the dashboard screen.**

The new DCT transmission was a revelation, and came with this very simple control lever on the centre console and paddle-shifts behind the steering wheel.

Red needles and M branding on the rev counter are here matched by a large red 'P' to remind the driver that this DCT car has its transmission in Park.

Six gears were not enough; BMW wanted to narrow the gap between ratios to ensure that gear changes could be as seamless as possible, and so they introduced their new two-pedal gearbox for the M3 as a seven-speed type. Manufactured for them by Getrag, it incorporated a Borg Warner DualTronic twin-clutch module, and came with the name of M-DKG in Germany; the letters stood for M Dop-pel-Kupplungs-Getriebe, which stood quite literally for M Double-Clutch Transmission, and that was the name given to it in English. In English-speaking countries, it was generally known as the M-DCT type, or more commonly simply as the DCT.

The new DCT transmission became available from April 2008 as an alternative to the existing six-speed manual gearbox. While it did not win over every M3 customer (and there were those who thought that an M3 was not a proper M3 without a manual gearbox), it delivered faster gear changes than even the best drivers could achieve with a manual 'box. They were smoother too. Left in fully automatic mode, the DCT gearbox knocked 0.2 seconds off the 0–100km/h (0–62mph) acceleration times of every M3 model then available. There could have been no better demonstration of its excellence.

OUT OF STEP: THE FIRST FACELIFT (2008)

As the earliest of the E90-series range to enter production, it was the four-door models of the 3 Series that became due

for a facelift first. As the two-door models with their different front ends had been introduced later and were therefore perceived as being more modern, BMW felt that it could leave them alone until later. So it was that the four-door models were revitalized in September 2008 for the 2009 model year and the M3 saloons were, of course, affected as well.

BMW's internal name for the facelift went by the bizarre English name of Life Cycle Impulse, and the facelifted cars were known as LCI types – a name which enthusiasts sometimes use but which did not catch on among buyers generally. The key changes were to the front and rear bumpers, while headlamps took on LED turn signals and a small 'eyebrow' like that on other recent models, and the rear lamp units reverted to the L-shape seen on earlier BMWs. Changes to the bonnet for the mainstream cars were nevertheless not reflected on the M3s, which retained their special aluminium panels with the 'power dome' to clear the V8 engine. Door mirrors changed, and so did some of the dashboard controls.

The iDrive system was also updated with what BMW called a Car Infotainment Computer (or CIC for short). This featured an 80GB hard drive, which took care of the satellite navigation system and could store 8GB of music files as well. These could be uploaded by way of a USB port in the glove compartment. The new system also had integral internet access, and was able to play DVD videos when the gear lever was in Neutral or (in the case of the DCT) in Park.

FACELIFTED TWO-DOORS AND THE COMPETITION PACKAGE (2010)

The two-door E90-series models had arrived some eighteen months after the four-door types, and with perfect Teutonic logic they were facelifted eighteen months after the four-doors had been facelifted. The changes affected all varieties of the Coupé and Convertible, and were introduced at the Geneva Motor Show in March 2010, but the changes for the M3 models were unique to them. There was also more than a cosmetic facelift: the arrival of M3 derivatives of the E92 LCI and E93 LCI models was accompanied by mechanical changes that focused on improving fuel economy and exhaust emissions, and was followed by the introduction of a new optional Competition Package.

Like the other two-door 3 Series models, the M3 took on new front and rear details, in particular new headlamps. Associated changes brought a new design of front apron, with carbon-fibre-look splitters in the outer vent sections. There was a restyled rear apron and diffuser, and an associated effect of the front and rear changes was to make the cars look slightly longer from the side, as if the front and rear overhangs had been lengthened. At the rear, the M3s took on the same new rear light units as the other LCI two-door models. Though fitting into the same space as the earlier type, these had glass covers over banks of LEDs that gave the tail lights a distinctive visual signature when illuminated in the dark. It was a satisfying detail that was right on target for M3 buyers.

The economy and emissions improvements came from BMW's Efficient Dynamics programme, which was being rolled out across the company's whole car range. Every car already had Brake Energy Regeneration, and now all M3s with the six-speed manual gearbox came with an Optimum Shift Indicator that told the driver when to change gear for maximum fuel efficiency. Most surprising to many onlookers, who did not associate the M3 with fuel saving measures, all cars were now also equipped with an automatic Start-Stop system that shut the engine down when the car was stationary (as occurs in heavy traffic or at traffic lights) and automatically restarted it as soon as the driver pressed the accelerator pedal. A system of electronic checks and balances ensured that there were no unwanted shutdowns, that the battery always had sufficient charge to restart the engine when required, and that the system was as unobtrusive in operation as possible. It was nevertheless quite a new experience for M3 drivers to sit at traffic lights with the engine off, and then rocket away in the usual fashion when they turned green.

The arrival of the Competition Package lagged slightly behind that of the LCI facelift for the two-doors. Announced in April 2010 as an option for the M3, it was made available only for the Coupé models. It was less far-reaching than the Competition Package that had been offered for the earlier E46 M3s, but nevertheless sharpened the focus of the M3 as a driver's car. It brought with it two cosmetic touches: 19-inch forged-alloy wheels, in the same style as those used on the E46 M3 CSL, and carbon-fibre-look elements in the front apron. In the UK, it was launched at a cost of £3,315, at a time when the standard M3 Coupé cost £53,275.

The changes to the suspension hardware were essentially the same as those seen on the M3 Edition a year earlier

(see Chapter 9). They brought shorter springs that had the same rates as the standard type, with dampers that had been recalibrated to suit.

However, there had been more extensive changes to the suspension's software. The Sport mode of the Electronic Damper Control system was made stiffer to improve cornering during track work – although it had a negative effect on ride comfort on the road. There were also changes to the M Dynamic Mode of the DSC system. Renamed Dynamic Traction Control or DTC, it allowed the tail to slide further in heavy cornering before intervening to help the driver regain control. When it did intervene, it worked differently from the standard system, which was programmed to cut the power to the wheels. Instead, the DTC focused on preventing a spin by braking individual wheels as necessary.

AN ENLARGED V8, 2010

BMW's M division was gradually working towards an entry in the Deutsche Tourenwagen Meisterschaft (DTM, or German Touring Car Championship), and as part of that programme it began to focus more specifically on competition derivatives of the M3. The whole programme was really designed to re-establish the M3's credentials as a competition car, as there was a growing feeling among enthusiasts and commentators alike that the M3 had been resting on the laurels earned by the original E30 model for far too long. There had been no M3 in major European competition since 1992, and BMW were determined to put that right.

In the meantime, the M division developed an enlarged 4.4-litre version of the V8 engine that was made available in a pair of competition-oriented M3 'specials'. These were the M3 GTS, a hardcore lightweight racing coupé that became available in May 2010, and the M3 CRT, another lightweight special that arrived in June 2011. Both of these cars were very different from the mainstream M3s, and both are discussed in more detail in Chapter 9.

EVOLUTION BY EDITIONS, 2011 TO 2013

The M3 did eventually go racing, as a silhouette car in the DTM during 2012, and was immediately a winner. But back in the showrooms, BMW had embarked on a quite different programme that they hoped would keep the cars fresh in the public imagination for the next two to three years. The plan was for the E90-series M3s to be replaced early in 2014, but the efforts of the M division were now being quite seriously stretched as demand arose for M versions of some of BMW's newer models, such as the X5 and X6. This made it difficult for the E90-series models to be developed any further. Besides, a great deal of development time was also being spent on the car that would eventually replace the existing M3.

Just as had happened with the E90-series cars, the forthcoming 3 Series was to be introduced in two stages – but there was a twist. Only the four-door models would be badged as 3 Series, and the forthcoming two-door derivatives would take on the new name of 4 Series. So the replacements for the M3 Coupés and Convertibles would logically be badged as M4s, and only the four-door Saloon model would carry on the legendary M3 name.

Amid the flurry of comment that inevitably accompanied this knowledge as it spread around M3 customers and enthusiasts, BMW also had to contend with a potential problem. This was that the new 3 Series range, coded F30, would be introduced in October 2012. The new shape would inevitably take some of the lustre away from the M3s that retained the old E90-series looks. BMW's solution to all these difficulties was to embark on an extended series of limited and special editions that would keep the M3 fresh until its replacement reached the showrooms.

The special-edition era had actually begun in June 2010, when US customers were offered the Frozen Gray edition, which mainly showcased one of the new matt-finish paints from BMW Individual. These 'Frozen' paints would feature on several more special editions over the next three years – the M Performance Edition for the UK in June 2012, and Frozen Silver Editions or Frozen Editions for several

ABOVE AND FAR OPPOSITE: **The very last E92 M3 was built in July 2013. Here it is during the build process, carrying 'Letzter E92' (Last E92) identification.**

countries that same summer. Then there were the Limited Edition 500 for the UK in July 2012, the DTM Champion Edition for Germany in February 2013 (celebrating the M3's DTM win in 2012) and the Lime Rock Park Edition for the USA in summer 2013. On top of that, there were several special editions designed specifically for the emerging Chinese market.

All these special-edition cars are examined in more detail in Chapter 9, and all of them have their own special interest for M3 enthusiasts. It must be said, however, that during these last few years of E90-series M3 production there was a growing feeling in the automotive world than BMW were expecting rather a lot of M3 buyers by not offering them anything that was really new. There was nothing wrong with the M3 as it stood, but was it wise for BMW to trade on the fact for so long? A glance at the production totals for the E90-series cars also makes clear that they were not selling in the same quantities as their predecessors; perhaps the M3 image was fading, and perhaps that change of designation to M4 on the 3 Series replacements from the M division would inject a new vitality to BMW's long-standing performance model.

Production of the E90-series M3s began to wind down in October 2011, when the last of the Saloon versions was built. Convertibles remained in low-volume production until September 2013, but BMW had already marked the end of the series by highlighting the production of the final E92 Coupé. Built on 5 July 2013 at the Regensburg plant, the car had left-hand drive, was finished in eye-catching Fire Orange paint, and was shipped to a dealer in Belgium.

Applying the BMW roundel and the M3 badge were two of the final assembly operations, carried out when the car was virtually complete.

COLOURS AND TRIMS FOR E90-SERIES M3 MODELS

Paint

The standard paint colours were as follows:

Alpine White	Melbourne Red
Interlagos Blue (by 2012)	Mineral White (not Saloons) (by 2012)
Jerez Black	Silverstone II
Jet Black (by 2012)	Space Grey (added by 2012)
Le Mans Blue (added by 2012)	

The BMW Individual paint options included the following:

Aegean Blue	Malachite Green Dark
Atlantic Blue	Michigan Blue
Atlantis	Midnight Blue
Aventurine Silver	Monaco Blue
Azurite Black	Montego Blue
Blue Onyx	Moonstone
Blue Water	Mora

Brass	Olivine
Carbon Black	Opal Black
Coloured Gold	Orient Blue
Dakar Yellow	Oxford Green II
Deep Green	Petrol Mica
Diamond	Phoenix Yellow
Diopside Black	Ruby Black
Fir Green	Ruby Red II
Flamenco Red	Santorini Blue II
Frozen Black (from 2010)	Sepia
Frozen Blue (from 2012)	Silver Grey
Frozen Gray (from 2010)	Steel Blue
Frozen Polar Silver (from 2010)	Sterling Grey
Frozen Red (from 2010)	Stratus Grey
Frozen Silver (from 2010)	Sydney Blue
Frozen White (from 2012)	Techno Violet
Grey Green	Titanium Grey II
Havana	Toledo Blue
Imola Red	Tourmaline Violet
Light Yellow	Velvet Blue

Upholstery

Upholstery was in leather as standard. Convertibles had leather with SunReflective Technology.

Novillo leather was available in Bamboo Beige, Black, Fox Red and Palladium Silver, and Extended Novillo leather was available in the same colours.

Individual Novillo leather was available in Champagne, Platinum and Rust Brown.

Interior trim

The trims available were Aluminium Shadow (4MX), Anthracite mirror-finish wood (4MZ), Black carbon-structure leather (4MY) and Titanium Shadow (771).

From the BMW Individual catalogue could be ordered Anthracite Maple wood (XE2), Piano Black with inlay (XEB) and Red Brown Eucalyptus (XE3).

PERFORMANCE FIGURES FOR E90-SERIES M3 MODELS

Coupé	0–62mph	4.8 sec with six-speed gearbox
	0–60mph	4.3 sec (*Motor Trend* test of six-speed model, 2008)
	0–62mph	4.6 sec with DCT gearbox
	0–60mph	3.9 sec (*Car and Driver* test of DCT model, 2011)
GTS Coupé	0–62mph	3.6 sec

Convertible	0–62mph	5.3 sec with six-speed gearbox
	0–62mph	5.1 sec with DCT gearbox

All cars had an electronic speed limiter that theoretically limited maximum speed to 250km/h (155mph). With the limiter removed, *Car and Driver* magazine claimed a maximum of 203mph (327km/h).

E90-SERIES M3 SPECIFICATIONS

Engines:

4.0-litre
Type S65B40 V8 petrol
3999cc (92mm × 75.2mm)
Twin overhead camshafts, chain-driven
Double-VANOS (variable valve timing on inlet and exhaust
  camshafts)
Four valves per cylinder
Seven-bearing crankshaft
Compression ratio 12.0:1
Siemens MSS 60 engine-management system
Catalytic converter standard
420PS at 8,300rpm
400Nm (295lb ft) at 3,900rpm

4.4-litre
Type S65B44 V8 petrol
4361cc (92mm × 82mm)
Twin overhead camshafts, chain-driven
Double-VANOS (variable valve timing on inlet and exhaust
  camshafts)
Four valves per cylinder
Seven-bearing crankshaft
Compression ratio 12.0:1
Siemens MSS 60 engine-management system
Catalytic converter standard
450PS at 8,300rpm
435Nm (321lb ft) at 3,900rpm

Transmission:
Six-speed manual gearbox
Ratios 4.06:1, 2.40:1, 1.58:1, 1.19:1, 1.00:1, 0.87:1, reverse
  3.68:1
Optional seven-speed M-DCT transmission with automatic
  clutch action
Ratios 4.780:1, 3.056:1, 2.153:1, 1.678:1, 1.390:1, 1.203:1,
  1.000:1, reverse 4.454:1

Axle ratio:
3.85:1 with six-speed manual gearbox
3.154:1 with M-DCT gearbox

Suspension, steering and brakes:
Front suspension with MacPherson struts, coil springs, Boge
  gas dampers and anti-roll bar
Rear suspension with five links, coil springs, Boge gas
  dampers and anti-roll bar
Rack-and-pinion steering with 12.5:1 ratio and standard
  Servotronic power assistance giving a variable degree of
  assistance dependent on speed
Ventilated compound-material disc brakes all round, 360mm
  (14.2in) on front wheels and 350mm (13.8in) on rear
  wheels (GTS with 378mm (14.9in) front discs and six-
  piston calipers, 380mm (15in) rear discs and four-piston
  calipers); twin hydraulic circuits; ABS standard

Dimensions:

Overall length:	2008–10 models	4,615mm (181.7in)
	2011–13 models	4,618mm (181.8in)
Overall width:	2008–10 models	1,804mm (71.0in)
	2011 Saloon	1,816mm (71.5in)
	2011–13 Coupé	1,821mm (71.7in)
	2011–13 Convertible	1,804mm (71.0in)
Overall height:	2008–10 Coupé	1,424mm (56.1in)
	2011–13 Coupé	1,412mm (55.6in)
	2008–10 Convertible	1,412mm (55.6in)
	2011–13 Convertible	1,392mm (54.8in)
	Saloon	1,448mm (57.0in)
Wheelbase:	2,761mm (108.7in)	
Front track:	1,540mm (60.6in)	
Rear track:	1,539mm (60.6in)	

Wheels and tyres:
Five-stud alloy wheels with 8.5in rims at the front and 9.5in
rims at the rear; 245/40R18 front tyres and 265/40R18 rear
tyres. 19-inch wheels optional

Kerb weights:

Coupé	1,655kg (3,649lb)
Saloon	1,605kg (3,538lb)
Convertible	1,880kg (4,145lb)

E90-SERIES M3 VIN CODES

All E90-series M3 models have a seventeen-digit Vehicle Identification Number (VIN). This consists of a ten-digit prefix and a seven-digit serial number. The VIN code is most easily read from a plate attached behind the lower edge of the windscreen.

A theoretical example would be:

WBSWD910X8E076543

which decodes as shown below. Alternatives for each position are shown in the right-hand column.

WBS	BMW Motorsport GmbH, Munich
WD	E92 Coupé, early
KG	E92 Coupé, late ('LCI')
VA	E90 Saloon, early
PM	E90 Saloon, late ('LCI')
WL	E93 Convertible (all 'LCI')
91	European specification, LHD
92	European specification, RHD
93	US specification, LHD

0	Standard placeholder code on European cars (On US cars, the number indicates the type of restraint system fitted)
X	Check digit (1–9, or X)
8	2008 model year

	9 = 2009	C = 2012	
	A = 2010	D = 2013	
	B = 2011		

E	Built at Regensburg
076543	Serial number

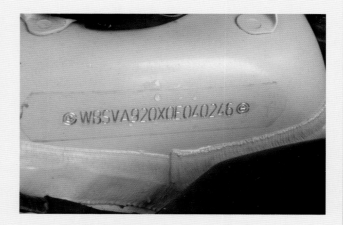

ABOVE: **The VIN is stamped on a suspension tower under the bonnet.**

LEFT: **The VIN is visible through the base of the windscreen, as demanded by law.**

PRODUCTION FIGURES FOR E90-SERIES M3 MODELS

Overall production totals are as follows:

Saloon	9,674
Coupé	40,092
Convertible	7,861 (to mid-2013)
Grand Total	57,627

Saloon production (E90)

2007–08 model years

Type	Manual gearbox	DCT gearbox	Total
RHD	436	164	600
LHD (Euro spec)	466	153	619
US spec	2,080	200	2,280
Total	2,982	517	**3,499**

2009–11 model years ('LCI' models)

Type	Manual gearbox	DCT gearbox	Total
RHD	135	1,174*	1,309
LHD (Euro spec)	146	1,133**	1,279
US spec	1,055	2,532	3,587
Total	1,336	4,839	**6,175**

* includes 5 M3 CRT models
** includes 63 M3 CRT models

Coupé production (E92)

2007–08 model years

Type	Manual gearbox	DCT gearbox	Total
RHD	3,309	2,193	5,502
LHD (Euro spec)	4,629	3,933	8,562
US spec	3,707	3,793	7,500
Total	11,645	9,919	**21,564**

2009–13 model years ('LCI' models)

Type	Manual gearbox	DCT gearbox	Total
RHD	300	3,716*	4,016
LHD (Euro spec)	293	5,920**	6,213
US spec	2,528	5,771	8,299
Total	3,121	15,407	**18,528**

* includes 25 M3 GTS models
** includes 113 M3 GTS models

Convertibles (E93)

(These totals are incomplete and show the figures up to July 2013 only.)

2009–13 model years

Type	Manual gearbox	DCT gearbox	Total
RHD	222	1,331	1,553
LHD (Euro spec)	255	2,047	2,302
US spec	1,955	2,051	4,006
Total	2,432	5,429	**7,861**

CHAPTER NINE

SPECIAL EDITIONS OF THE E90-SERIES M3

In the second half of the E90-series M3's production life, BMW exploited the appeal of special-edition models to what some commentators thought was the limit – or maybe even beyond. There was no doubt that the special editions did offer a degree of exclusivity because they were made in limited numbers, and exclusivity has always been an important factor in the appeal of the M3. Nevertheless, it was hard not to see some of these limited-run models as little more than showcases for items from the BMW Individual range that could be added to a standard M3 if a customer so wished.

Yet it would be wrong to be unduly cynical about the special editions. They did include some genuinely special models, notably the GTS and CRT with their enlarged V8 engines, and the run of Pure editions for Australia with their back-to-basics specification. These special editions also included a select group of bespoke models for the emerging Chinese market, where the M3 picked up a new and enthusiastic following.

THE M3 EDITION (2009)

The excitement of the new has been an essential part of the M3 ever since the E36 turned it into an everyday useable machine rather than a thinly disguised race car in 1992. The facelift for the two-door models of the E90 series was scheduled for the first quarter of 2010, which left quite a long gap after the 2008 saloon facelift. So the M division decided to fill it with what it called the M3 Edition, announced in July 2009 and to all intents and purposes a 2010-model-year car.

The M3 Edition was a Coupé and was available in just four colours: Alpine White, Black, Dakar Yellow and Monte Carlo Blue, of which the latter two were exclusive to the

new model. All the cars came with dark 'eloxy' plating for the grilles, wing vents and tailpipe tips, and with distinctive black caps on the door mirrors. The 19-inch Double-Spoke alloy wheels were also black, although the standard finish was available for those who asked.

The door sill strips had a chequered flag design and the M3 logo, and the seats were upholstered in black Novillo 'carbon structure' leather with contrasting stitching to match the exterior paint, and with vertical trim stripes on the upper backrest and the front of the cushion. On Black cars, the leather had white stitching, and both Black and Alpine White cars came with white centre and door armrests and a white centre console.

Essentially, then, the M3 Edition was a cosmetic makeover for the Coupé – but for one thing. BMW's M division had reduced the car's ride height by 10mm. This, according to some of those who drove one, made a difference to the car's handling that was quite out of proportion to the tiny

The special upholstery and trim of the 2009 M3 Edition can be seen in this picture of a RHD car.

amount it appeared to be. The car tested by *Evo* magazine in its November 2009 issue came with Continental Sport Contact 3 tyres instead of the usual Michelin Pilot Sport Cup types, and these seemed to help the transformation. But BMW were already one step ahead, and just a year later they would introduce a lowered ride height as part of the optional Competition Package (*see* Chapter 8).

THE M3 GTS (2010)

BMW made no bones about the way they saw the M3 GTS special edition, describing it in an early press release as 'offering a genuine motor sport driving experience in every respect'. The car was announced in November 2009, the launch proper was in spring 2010, cars were available in Germany from May and there were examples for other European countries from that summer. BMW let members of the motoring media loose with the M3 GTS at the Ascari track in Spain at the beginning of July 2010.

However, the M3 GTS was a European-specification car only, and none of those built was intended for sale in North America. Bizarrely, the build total remains in dispute: some argue for 250 examples, while others argue for 135 or 137 (the latter figure presumably representing 135 plus two pre-production samples). Of those, either fifteen or twenty-five were built with right hand-drive for the UK during January and February 2011. The word from BMW was that every single example of the GTS had already been sold before any of them actually reached dealers' showrooms.

ALSO OVERLEAF: **Experts still argue about the number of M3 GTS cars built. The car was an E92 Coupé, intended for competition enthusiasts – and nobody could miss that Fire Orange paint job.**

TOP: **The adjustable rear spoiler on the M3 GTS was not just for show. It allowed an owner to vary downforce at the rear to suit different race tracks.**

BELOW: **The M3 GTS came complete with racing seats and safety harnesses, a roll cage and even a fire extinguisher.**

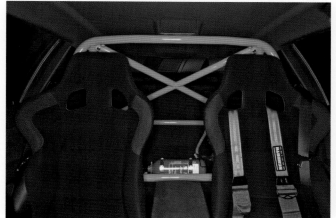

The GTS was a very special car indeed, and its price tag (including VAT) of £115,215 in Britain made it some £60,000 more expensive than a standard M3 – or a little less than twice the price. At that price, buyers wanted a car that looked special too, and BMW did not disappoint. The GTS was instantly recognizable by its tall, racing-style adjustable rear spoiler, based on that seen on the 320Si that BMW had been racing in the World Touring Car Championships. The car came with a special front air dam with adjustable air guidance vanes, and the BMW grille and wing side vents were finished in a special dark 'eloxy' plating.

A quick look inside would reveal that the GTS had no rear seat. That had been sacrificed to save weight, and occupying a sizeable proportion of the space behind the front bucket seats was a tubular rollover bar with sturdy bracing. Steering wheel, door and side panels were trimmed in Alcantara, and the car came with track-oriented extras: six-point seat belts, a fire extinguisher and preparation for an emergency off-switch.

The real heart of the GTS was, however, its new 4.4-litre V8 engine, developed from the 4.0-litre type in the standard-production M3. While the bore remained 92mm, the stroke went up to 82mm, boosting maximum power to 450PS and peak torque to 440Nm (325lb ft), the latter slightly lower down the rev range than on the 4.0-litre engine. BMW publicity claimed that the engine drew on motor sport experience. As for the performance available, it was simply enormous: the M3 GTS could reach 100km/h (62mph) from a standing start in 3.6 seconds, and needed just 7.8 seconds to reach 100mph from rest.

The only transmission on offer was a strengthened version of the seven-speed DCT type, with DKG Drivelogic. The usual centre selector was present, but the racing-style paddle shifts behind the steering wheel were much more likely to get regular use. Power was put down through 19-inch Double-Spoke M light-alloy Competition wheels, running on Pirelli P Zero Corsa racing tyres as standard, with a 255/35R19 size at the front and 285/30R19s at the rear.

There were no half measures in the chassis either. The rear sub-frame was bolted firmly into place for additional stiffness, and all four dampers could be adjusted to give the optimum bump and rebound strokes for the track where the car was being driven. The fixed-caliper brakes had six pistons each on the front wheels and four pistons each on the rear pair, and the discs had a 378mm (14.9in) diameter at the front with a 32mm (1.3in) width and a 380mm (15in) diameter at the rear with a narrower 28mm (1.1in) width. Then the DSC came with a race-oriented calibration, which was more tolerant of wheelspin than the standard system.

Weight saving had been central to the development programme, too. The M3 GTS weighed just 1,490kg (3,285lb) in standard trim, saving around 136kg (300lb) as compared to the standard M3. Side and rear windows were made of perspex, and even the exhaust system was made of lightweight (and expensive) titanium. The centre console and door trims were made of carbon fibre to save weight and, of course, a reduced level of sound insulation and the absence of rear seats made their own contribution. Yet this was not a completely spartan car, and BMW's M division had fitted it with a special audio system (lightweight, of course) and automatic air conditioning; drivers were expected to be comfortable on their way to track-day events.

THE M3 FROZEN GRAY EDITION (2010)

Matt-finish paints were a relatively new phenomenon in the custom and modified car scene, and BMW espoused them with enthusiasm at the end of the 2000s, offering them as extra-cost options from BMW Individual. They were also used on several special- and limited-edition models of the M3 from 2010, and many of these were released in several countries at more or less the same time but with variations to suit the individual markets.

The matt paint finishes were achieved by applying a BMW-developed silk matt clear coat over the coloured metallic base coat. BMW baptised them 'Frozen' finishes, and claimed that they met or exceeded all its standards for durability and longevity. (The company's English-language publicity material also usually described them as 'matte' finishes, using the preferred American English spelling of the word.) They did come with certain conditions, however, and the standard factory warranty was subject to strict observation of these. Traditional polishing was strictly forbidden, and all surface contaminants had to be removed quickly and carefully in case they left glossy patches on the paint. However, they were also attention grabbers, and BMW knew that this would appeal to the buyers of models from its M division.

The earliest of the myriad 'Frozen' special editions was announced in June 2010 as a 2011 model for the USA. Marketing linked it to the twenty-fifth anniversary of the M3 that would occur during 2011, and suggested that it might be a run-out model for the E92 Coupé. As US buyers were to discover, however, there was more life in the E92 than they might have expected, and they would be offered several more special editions that might (or might not) be the last ones available. This first one was called the Frozen Gray Edition, and BMW North America built a cautious total of thirty cars. (Again, the favoured US spelling of 'gray' was used rather than 'grey', which would be used on later models for the UK.)

All the Frozen Gray cars had the seven-speed DCT transmission and the then-new Competition Package of lowered suspension, reprogrammed electronic dampers with a Sport mode, and a less intrusive DSC stability control. They were equipped as standard with both the Premium Package and the Technology Package, the former consisting of power-folding mirrors, BMW Assist, a garage-door opener and carbon-fibre-look trim with leather upholstery, while the latter brought M Drive, keyless ignition, the iDrive navigation system with traffic information and voice recognition.

The upholstery was in black and red leather, with heated front seats, and an upgraded audio system included satellite radio and iPod connectivity. Park Distance Control was also standard, and the asking price of $78,900 (only some

$4,000 more than a similarly equipped standard M3 Coupé at the time) included a day at the BMW Performance Driving School in South Carolina.

THE M3 TIGER EDITION (2010)

The massive expansion of the Chinese economy in the first decade of the twenty-first century presented western car makers with huge opportunities, and many put in a great deal of effort to exploit these at a time when the west was suffering from an economic downturn that had begun in 2008. BMW was among them, and in the first half of 2010 reported that its overall sales in China had more than doubled compared with the same period in 2009.

So it was no great surprise when BMW introduced a special edition of the M3 destined only for the Chinese market. This was announced at the end of August 2010 and was called the M3 Tiger Edition, a name chosen to indicate that it was introduced during the Year of the Tiger, which ran from February 2010 to February 2011.

The car seems to have been rather hastily prepared over the summer of 2010, as it was not introduced at the Beijing Motor Show in April 2010, which would have been the ideal showcase for it. The exterior of the 250-strong Tiger Edition was based on that of the M3 GTS, with the same Fire Orange paint and contrasting black and dark chrome body highlights, and black 19-inch wheels. However, the Tiger Edition was otherwise a very different car. Unlike all other M3 Coupés at the time, it dispensed with the lightweight carbon-fibre roof panel, and instead had a steel roof with the glass sunroof that Chinese buyers wanted. It also had a proper rear seat.

Opening the doors revealed 'Tiger Edition' logos on the sill kick plates, black Novillo leather upholstery with orange contrast stitching, and an orange tiger's head embroidered on each front seat headrest. The Tiger Edition was mechanically standard, with the 420PS V8 engine and a DCT gearbox.

THE M3 PURE EDITION (2011)

BMW Australia adopted an interesting marketing tactic in January 2011 with the introduction of a back-to-basics special edition called the M3 Pure Edition. There were fifty Coupés and fifty Saloons, all sold at a price well below that of the standard M3 thanks to deletion of a number of luxury

The Pure Edition in 2011 was an Australian-market special that went down very well.

items. What was left was much appreciated by enthusiasts as the real essence of M3. All cars had the standard 4.0-litre V8 engine, with a six-speed manual gearbox.

The Coupés did without the otherwise standard carbon-fibre roof, and absent from all 100 cars were the driver-selectable features of the M Drive system. Only the Power button remained, to select a sharper throttle response. The adaptive headlights, alarm, CD changer, front seat heaters, Keyless-Go system and power-fold door mirrors were also deleted, and the seats were upholstered in cloth-and-leather instead of full leather.

There were just two standard paint colours – Alpine White or Black, although buyers could pay extra for metallic colours from the standard colour range. All 100 cars came with 19-inch M Double-Spoke wheels in high-gloss black, a high-gloss black bonnet air intake, and dark chrome grille, side vents and exhaust tips.

All 100 of these cars were said to have sold out in record time, and to have boosted Australian M3 sales by almost 10 per cent in 2011.

THE M3 MATTE EDITION (2011)

The Tiger Edition in 2010 was a sell-out success, and so BMW swiftly followed up with a second special edition for China. Introduced in March 2011, the M3 Matte Edition was again available only in China, and was an otherwise standard M3 Coupé with DCT gearbox finished in matt gunmetal grey or black, with black or dark chrome highlights, high-gloss metal-finish wheels and contrasting red brake calipers. This time, the standard M3 Coupé's carbon-fibre roof panel was fitted.

China was an important new market for the M3, and in 2011 was treated to the Matte Edition, which featured 'frozen' paints from the BMW Individual range.

The Matte Edition's interior featured upholstery in black 'carbon-look' leather with red stitching. There were carbon-fibre trim panels on the dashboard, centre console and doors, and a BMW Performance gear selector grip.

THE M3 CRT (2011)

The M3 CRT introduced in 2011 was another sell-out before it reached the showrooms, and was announced immediately before the Nürburgring 24 Hours event that took place on 25–26 June. Every one of the sixty-seven cars built had a deposit on it before the model was launched as a 2012-model-year car. This time, the special edition was based on the saloon version of the M3, and it was this that ensured there would be no imports for the UK market. BMW in the UK believed that their customers saw the M3 primarily as a Coupé and a Convertible; M3 Saloon sales were minimal and so, they believed, a special-edition saloon would not sell. They may have been right, because the CRT was a formidably expensive car, even though its showroom price was around 10 per cent less than that of an M3 GTS.

The initials CRT stood for Carbon Racing Technology, and the new model provided an interesting insight into the synergies between mainstream BMW production and the special cars developed by the M division. Its bonnet, front seats and rear spoiler were made of a new lightweight material called CFRP (Carbon Fibre Reinforced Plastic), which had been developed primarily for BMW's forthcoming i3 and i8 electric cars, and was claimed to weigh around a quarter of the steel equivalent. The old adage of 'race on Sunday, sell on Monday' clearly still applied, although BMW's press release for the M3 CRT expressed it in different words: 'bred for the race track but registered for the road' was the way the English-language version put it. One benefit was to the weight distribution of the car, and BMW claimed that 48.4 per cent of the weight was now over the rear wheels – slightly more than in the standard M3 saloon and resulting in greater agility.

Not surprisingly, the mechanical specification of the M3 CRT was very similar to that of the M3 GTS. The two cars shared the new 4.4-litre V8 engine in the same state of tune with its lightweight titanium exhaust, the same Drivelogic DCT gearbox and the same rigidly mounted rear subframe

A special rear diffuser and unique boot lip spoiler were part of the CRT specification.

TOP AND MIDDLE: **The M3 CRT of 2011 was another track-focused car, this time based on the E90 saloon.**

BOTTOM: **The CRT's competition orientation did not prevent BMW from adorning it with the special details that M3 buyers love, such as red highlights on the wing vents and bonnet vents.**

TOP: **Like the earlier GTS, the M3 CRT had an enlarged V8 engine of 4.4 litres.**

BELOW: **Uniquely finished elements in the interior and on the sill kick plates added to the special appeal of the M3 CRT. It was almost too good to use in anger on a race track.**

**The CRT's special dashboard trim carried
a numbered limited-edition plate.**

and adjustable dampers to sharpen the handling. The brakes were the same fixed-caliper type with six pistons at the front, Stahlflex brake lines and special pads. Yet this was less of a hardcore competition model than the M3 GTS and more of a showcase for the new technology. It actually had rear seats, and it came as standard with BMW's Professional satellite-navigation system, a BMW Individual high-specification audio system, and Park Distance Control front and rear. For all that, the new lightweight construction materials made it 45kg (99lb) lighter than a standard M3 saloon and 70kg (154lb) lighter than an M3 with a similar level of equipment.

The CRT models all had a distinctive front apron, and all of them came in Frozen Polar Silver matt-finish paint with Melbourne Red highlights on the bonnet and a discreet lip spoiler on the boot lid. The wheels were 19-inch alloys with a Y-spoke design, and were finished in black. They carried road-biased tyres instead of the track-biased Pirellis of the M3 GTS, with 245/35R19s at the front and 265/35R19s at the rear.

There were other distinctive touches inside the passenger cabin. Grained aluminium was used for the door sill strips, the door panels and the trim strips, and each car had a plaque on the dashboard that carried its individual number within the limited edition. The seats, which included a special individual rear pair that were similar to those in the front, were all upholstered in striking Sakhir Orange and Black, and the steering wheel had an Alcantara-trimmed rim and, of course, incorporated the M Drive button. There was even a racing package with the car that included a helmet.

THE M3 FROZEN BLACK EDITIONS (2011)

BMW followed up the success of the Frozen Gray Edition by a similar special edition for the USA a year later. The Frozen Black Edition of twenty cars was based on the M3 Coupé, equipped with the standard 4.0-litre V8 engine driving through the DCT transmission. The Frozen Black cars came with the Competition Package as standard equipment and cost $79,650 each. They became available in June 2011 as 2012 models.

Mostly, though, the Frozen Black Edition was about appearances. BMW stressed this in publicity material, which claimed that, 'compared to conventional exterior colours with gloss finish, the sculpture-like character of Frozen Black paint highlights the athletic contours of the M3.' Gloss black exterior trim and gloss black 19-inch wheels as used on the M3 GTS were complemented by red-painted brake calipers. Inside, the cabin boasted black Novillo leather upholstery with red contrast stitching, the Enhanced Premium Sound System from BMW Individual and a collection of other items that were normally extra-cost options. BMW North America added to the interest by saying that the first nineteen cars would go on sale immediately but that they would hold on to the twentieth, which might be sold at a later date.

The interest that this special edition generated persuaded BMW in Australia to request a similar one, and towards the end of 2012 there was a Frozen Black Edition in that country too. It consisted of just twelve cars, all with the right-hand drive demanded by that market.

THE M3 CARBON EDITION (2011)

Exploiting the new interest from China for the M3, BMW introduced a third special edition exclusive to that market in June 2011. The M3 Carbon Edition consisted of 111 Coupés with the standard engine specification and DCT gearbox but with a number of special cosmetic features.

All the cars were painted in Mineral White, with a black stripe running along the wing tops between headlights and windscreen pillar. Each door carried a 'Carbon Edition' decal, together with the Motorsport logo. Standard carbon-fibre roofs were fitted, together with a carbon-fibre body kit and rear spoiler, black wheels and high-gloss chrome exterior trim. The interiors had black leather with contrasting white stitching.

THE M3 COMPETITION EDITION (2011)

In November 2011, BMW USA issued a new special edition of the M3 Coupé, which was marketed as a celebration of forty years of the BMW M cars. There were, appropriately, forty examples, all with the standard 4.0-litre V8 engine driving through a DCT transmission, and all finished in Frozen Silver metallic paint from the BMW Individual options list. Black bonnet air intakes, black M3 GTS-style wheels, and dark chrome grilles, wing vents and exhaust tips were all standard.

On the inside, there was black Extended Novillo Leather with unique palladium silver accents and palladium silver contrast stitching on front seats, headrests, door trim panels, centre console and centre armrest. The interior was further distinguished with an Alcantara-covered multi-function M steering wheel with an M3 chequered flag logo inlay. The door sill kick plates also featured the chequered flag logo while the handbrake lever carried an embroidered M Power logo. The dash and centre console had genuine carbon-fibre trim elements.

As the special edition's name suggested, the Competition Package with its lowered ride height was part of the standard equipment. These cars were also used as a 'reward' for US BMW dealers, and one was allocated to each of the first forty dealers to become M Certified Centers – which involved meeting certain standards set by BMW USA. The Competi-tion Edition cars were sold as 2012 models, and are generally known as such among BMW enthusiasts in the USA.

THE M3 PURE EDITION II (2012)

The success of the first Pure Edition persuaded BMW Australia to issue a second in March 2012, this time consisting of just fifty cars, all Coupés. The Pure Edition II was largely the same as the earlier model, with a stripped-out specification but high-gloss black and dark chrome exterior highlights. The main differences were in the exterior colour selection, which now included Fire Orange (first seen on the M3 GTS), Dakar Yellow II, Imola Red, Laguna Seca and Sepang Bronze. Interior features included a handbrake gaiter with 'M Power' stitching and sill kick plates with a chequered flag inlay.

THE M3 M PERFORMANCE EDITION (2012)

The UK market was treated to a pair of special editions from the M division in June 2012, neither of which was available anywhere else. Both were called M Performance Editions and both were of thirty cars only. There was one for the M5 and one for the M3, based on the Coupé.

The M3 M Performance Edition deliberately showcased some of the options available from BMW Individual, the

LEFT AND OPPOSITE:
Buyers of the 2012 M Performance Edition for the UK market had a choice of red, white and blue – all 'Frozen' colours.

'One of 30' it says – but one day buyers will want to know exactly where it fitted into the build sequence.

marketing idea being that buyers who could not quite stretch to the £74,080 base price of the special edition might at least choose some of its special options for a less expensive standard-production M3. So despite the suggestion that the name carried, the M Performance Edition was more about cosmetics than about performance. In fact, it came with the standard 420PS engine and seven-speed DCT gearbox with variable M Differential; the only performance-oriented feature was the standard Competition Package of lowered suspension, Electronic Damper Control with Sport mode, and revised DSC+ system.

The thirty M Performance Edition cars brought BMW Individual's new matt-finish paints to public attention. So there were ten cars in Frozen Red, ten in Frozen White and ten in Frozen Blue – and more than one commentator at the time spotted the red, white and blue link with the Queen's Diamond Jubilee, which was celebrated in 2012.

LEFT AND ABOVE: **The M Performance Edition also featured interior options from the BMW Individual catalogue. Such details as the logo on the headrest and the coloured stitching were calculated to appeal to M3 enthusiasts.**

Standard on all thirty cars were matt black 19-inch Y-spoke alloy wheels and Jet Black bonnet air intakes. Dark Chrome was used for the grille surrounds, the wing vents and the exhaust tips, and there was high-gloss Shadowline trim. Carbon-fibre splitters added their own highlight to the front air dam. Tinted glass was standard, and so were folding door mirrors.

There were, as there had to be, some special interior features as well. So the door sills carried the legend 'BMW M Performance Edition', and the upholstery was in Black Novillo leather with contrast stitching in Mugello Red, Lotus White or Tobago Blue to match the exterior paint. The front seat headrests had M stitching, the floor mats had contrast piping, and the steering wheel had an Alcantara-trimmed rim. Interior trim was in Piano Black from the BMW Individual range, but uniquely carried the laser-cut designation 'One of 30'. This followed the latest thinking at BMW, which was to avoid numbering limited-edition cars individually. The somewhat lame excuse from the company was that this ensured no one car would be worth more than another because of its place within the limited edition. Perhaps they were right in the short term, but it is inconceivable that enthusiasts in the future will not try to establish the build order of the cars and so to work out which were the first and the last examples.

By the time of the Frozen Silver Edition in 2012, BMW had decided not to number cars within special editions; instead, each one of these was simply 'One of 100'. Although the special edition was for the UK and had RHD, BMW press material showed the interior of a LHD car!

Completing the special-equipment list were adaptive headlights and Park Distance Control front and rear. Inside, buyers were promised a sliding front armrest, heated front seats, a DAB digital radio with the thirteen-speaker Harman/Kardon system and a USB audio interface, the BMW Professional Media Package, mobile application preparation and internet connectivity. All this, and the special features drawn from the BMW Individual catalogue, was said to have a value of £9,790. As the car actually cost £16,075 more than a standard production M3 Coupé with the DCT gearbox, that made the price of exclusivity very high indeed.

THE FROZEN SILVER EDITIONS (2012–13)

The M division made good use of its new matt paint finishes over the summer of 2012. In addition to the M Performance Edition, the UK market was provided with a further 100-

car edition that went on sale in June that year as the Frozen Silver Edition.

In most respects, these cars had the same equipment specification as the M Performance Edition, with the Competition Pack as standard and the dark exterior trim. The most obvious difference was that they were painted in Frozen Silver and did not have the carbon-fibre splitter inserts in the front apron. The special-edition identification inside read 'One of 100', the M Performance Edition identifiers were absent, and the seats were in two-tone black and grey leather. Prices began at £58,720, which was just £4,000 more than a standard M3 Coupé and therefore considerably cheaper than the M Performance Edition.

In the USA, meanwhile, there was a Frozen Silver Edition alongside the 150 red, white and blue cars of the Frozen Edition (*see* below). Essentially similar to the Frozen Silver Edition in the UK, these cars became available in November 2012 as 2013 models and all of them had the DCT automatic gearbox. BMW marketed them as a special edition to commemorate forty years of BMW Motorsport racing in the USA, and as a result there were just forty cars. All of them had the cold-weather and premium packages as standard.

THE M3 PURE COUPÉ (2013)

The 'Pure' concept was such a success in Australia that it returned in January 2013 for a third time, priced at Aus$30,000 below the standard car's Aus$155,100 price tag. This time, only Coupés were available, and the edition was generally known simply as the Pure Coupé. There was no predetermined limit on the quantity available, although BMW Australia did point out that M3 production was scheduled to end some time in 2013 and that this would bring availability of the Pure Coupé to a close. The Australian cars were accompanied by an allocation of twenty similar examples for New Zealand.

As on earlier Pure editions for Australia, a number of features that did not affect performance and dynamics had been dropped in order to achieve the low showroom price. The Pure Coupé was nevertheless still well-equipped, with bi-xenon headlights, Professional satellite navigation, Bluetooth and USB connectivity, parking sensors and the carbon-fibre roof panel. BMW Australia also announced some quite major price reductions on option packs available from the standard range and applicable to the Pure Coupé as well.

THE M3 DTM CHAMPION EDITION (2013)

There was a strange air of inevitability about the M3 DTM Champion Edition that was announced in February 2013. That BMW should commemorate its 2012 DTM victory with a limited edition was just one part of it; the other was that the build should be limited to just fifty-four cars – the same number of events that M3s had won in the DTM series since their first appearance in the mid-1980s. Sadly, but unsurprisingly, all the cars were built with left-hand drive for the German domestic market.

None of that made the Champion Edition any less exciting, of course. Nor did the fact that it was based on the standard production Coupé bodyshell and therefore bore only the vaguest resemblance to the cars that had actually won all those victories in 2012. The car came in Frozen Black matt-finish paint, with matching wheels and dark chrome accents, and a tricolour M stripe running over the roof and rear deck, exactly as Bruno Spengler's car had on the tracks.

Lest onlookers should be in any doubt, the Champion Edition cars also had a large M decal logo behind each front wheel, and a Canadian flag on each rear side window with Bruno Spengler's name below it. Carbon flaps and gurney (the trailing edge flap) also suggested the real thing, but Park Distance Control was a reminder that this was fundamentally a civilized road-going car, even if it did have pretensions to look like the DTM winner.

The all-black interior was highlighted by a carbon-fibre plaque on the dashboard ahead of the passenger seat, with Spengler's signature and the legend 'DTM Champions 2012'. This plaque also carried the car's own individual number within its limited edition. There were carbon-fibre and Alcantara trim items, and the door sills were lined with the colours of the helmet that Spengler wore during the 2012 DTM. A neat touch was the 'M Power' embroidery on the handbrake grip. It was, however, a road car, and so the competition-style front seats had heating elements.

The car came with a number of extras that were extra-cost options on a standard M3, including the M3 Competition Package, M Drive, M DCT Drivelogic and the M Driver's Package. Then, as part of the €99,000 list price (equivalent to more than £80,000 in the UK at the time), buyers were offered a special 'BMW M Fascination Nordschleife' driver training course, in which Bruno Spengler himself would demonstrate the car's capabilities at the Nürburgring.

THE FROZEN EDITION (2012)

Even though the UK was alone in getting the M Performance Edition, the essence of those special cars was repeated in a contemporary limited edition for the USA. This was called the Frozen Edition, was released in October 2012 as a 2013-model-year option, and consisted of 150 cars. There were fifty cars in Frozen Red, fifty in Frozen White and fifty in Frozen Blue; this time, the red, white and blue theme played with the colours in the American flag.

As on the UK cars, the Competition Package was standard, together with the matt black wheels and the same Dark Chrome and Jet Black exterior trim items. The black Novillo leather upholstery and the other cabin accoutrements were unchanged, although the legends on the door sills and door

trims were different. Where the Frozen Edition did differ was in its inclusion of the six-speed manual transmission as standard, the dual-clutch automatic being only optional. Other extra-cost items were a cold-weather package, a sunroof, heated front seats and the top-specification audio system.

THE M3 LIMITED EDITION 500 (2012)

In Britain, BMW announced a special edition of 500 cars in July 2012 under the somewhat uninspired name of 'Limited Edition 500'. It came as both a Coupé and a Convertible, the fixed-roof car being priced from £55,690 and the open model from £59,785.

The M3 Limited Edition 500 was a 2012 run of 500 cars for the UK, featuring gloss paints instead of the 'Frozen' types so often used on special editions in this period.

There were no mechanical changes: the 4.0-litre V8 came in standard tune and customers could choose between the manual and DCT transmissions. However, the Limited Edition 500 cars did come with a suite of extras that would have cost £4,300 as options on a standard car but were included for a price premium of just £1,000.

The red, white and blue theme of the M Performance Edition had been successful, and so it was pursued for the Limited Edition 500 cars. However, this time the paints were not matt-finish types but rather three unique gloss colours called Imola Red, Mineral White and Santorini Blue. All were set off by gloss black 19-inch wheels, with Dark Chrome grille surrounds, wing vents and exhaust tips.

The upholstery on all 500 cars was in Novillo leather, with contrasting stitching on the seats, steering wheel and door trims. Red cars came with black leather and red stitching, white cars with red leather and black stitching, and blue cars with black leather and blue stitching. In each case, the trim was in Piano Black, with individually numbered Limited Edition details laser-cut into the dashboard.

THE FROZEN SILVER EDITION (2013)

Prompted by the success of earlier special-edition models, BMW Australia sold yet another limited edition in early 2013, called the Frozen Silver Edition. There were just ten of these cars, which, as the name suggests, were characterized by Frozen Silver paintwork. They were seen in Australia as a 'farewell' edition of the E92 M3 Coupé.

THE LIME ROCK PARK EDITION (2013)

The focus of motor sport activity on the DTM had meant that the M3's largest market in the USA had been denied any of the limited edition cars built between 2010 and 2012. So by way of compensation – or maybe even apology – BMW drew up a special edition of 200 cars for the USA to commemorate the end of E90-series M3 production in summer 2013. They called it the Lime Rock Park Edition, taking the name from the famous Connecticut speedway associated with NASCAR events. They even made sure that the car was tested there, and that it satisfied the demands of the speedway's owner, racing guru Skip Barber.

The power-train specification was essentially standard, with the 450PS (444bhp) 4.0-litre V8 exhausting through the lightweight titanium system that was not advertised to deliver extra power – but was claimed to give an extra 5bhp or so if bought as an optional extra for a standard M3. However, the key special feature of the Lime Rock Park Edition was that the speed limiter had been reset to allow the car to reach its natural maximum speed of 300km/h (186mph) – reason enough for enthusiasts to buy one, even if the only places in the USA where that speed could legally and safely be achieved were race tracks like Lime Rock Park itself.

Either the six-speed manual or the DCT gearbox could be ordered, and the steering ratio was quicker than standard, giving just two turns of the wheel from lock to lock. The ride height was lowered by 15mm (0.6in), and the car rode on Pirelli P-Zero tyres, with a 245 width at the front and a 265 width at the rear. The Competition Package was standard, and so was the competition-friendly version of the DSC with its later-than-standard intervention.

The front air dam had black carbon-fibre splitters and the rear spoiler was also made of carbon fibre as standard. Every example of the limited edition came in eye-catching Fire Orange paint with black Novillo leather upholstery, and every car had its own special-edition plaque and paper authentication certificate. As was by now normal (but not universal) BMW practice, the cars were not individually numbered, and the special-edition plaques all read 'One of 200'.

As was increasingly common when new limited editions of the M3 were launched, however, there were sceptics. Not every US BMW enthusiast could see the sense in a commemorative final edition that offered no more acceleration than the standard M3, even if it did have a particularly striking appearance. It must be said that they had a point.

CHAPTER TEN

DRIVING, BUYING AND COMPETITION WITH THE E90-SERIES M3

The original E30-based BMW M3 had been developed as a road-going version of the competition car, but ever since its demise in the early 1990s there had been mutterings of discontent in some quarters. Here, the argument ran that the M3 was no longer a tamed competition car but rather a slick, high-performance luxury machine that used the racing heritage of the original M3 as a marketing tool.

With the E90-series cars, BMW determined to restore the competition pedigree of the M3, and one result was that the focus of many special editions was on competition. If BMW never seriously expected every buyer of one of these cars to use it on the track at weekends, they could at least boast that every car was track-oriented, and that with a little preparation it could be used as a credible competition machine in Clubsport events.

All this gradually built up a fund of experience and expertise that led to the creation of competition M3s for the ALMS (American Le Mans Series) in 2009 and then for the DTM (Deutsche Tourenwagen Meisterschaft, or German Touring Car Championship) in 2012. BMW would not have announced an entry if they had not been pretty convinced that the car they had developed had a very good chance of winning – and win it did, straight out of the box in its first season, as explained later in this chapter.

THE M3 RETURNS TO COMPETITION

BMW simply had to get M3s back on the race tracks, and in practice it would not be long after the launch of the E90-

series cars that they did so. But for the first few years of the E90-series' production life, the teams they fielded in the World Touring Car Championships used E90 320Si models. In 2006 and 2007, BMW Team UK (again run by RBM) took Andy Priaulx to the drivers' title, but 2008 and 2009 were not so successful. For 2010, BMW reduced its WTCC presence, entering just two cars under BMW Team RBM with Andy Priaulx and Augusto Farfus as drivers. They finished third in the manufacturers' title.

Meanwhile, new plans were already being implemented. At the end of the 2006 race season, BMW North America parted company with its long-term race partner, Prototype Technology Group. In mid-2007, the first steps towards the development of a racing E92 M3 had been taken, and at the Chicago Auto Show in autumn 2008, BMW announced a racing version of the car that was designed to compete in the 2009 ALMS (American Le Mans Series) events – where engines were not restricted to the 2.0-litre capacity of the WTCC.

BMW Motorsport Director Mario Thiessen explained it like this for a press release of the time:

With the sporting genes of the production BMW M3 being clearly evident, developing a racing version of the car was the next logical step. The fact that the road-going vehicle is fitted with a V8 engine as standard provided us with an ideal base. However, the BMW M3 is more than a race car, it has achieved legendary status amongst race fans across the globe. I am convinced that this unique story of the BMW M3 racing cars will now be expanded upon by the addition of further chapters.

THE M3 GT4

GT4 class racing was introduced to provide a recognized international series for amateur drivers in Europe, using what were in effect production cars built to a standardized specification so that the focus was put on driver skill. The series was a sports car championship created and run by the Stéphane Ratel Organisation (SRO).

To meet demand, BMW announced a GT4 version of the M3 – in effect a factory-built race car available to privateers. The cars became available on 7 July 2009 at a cost of 121,500 Euros (plus VAT where applicable), and used standard engines in a car with an overall weight of 1,430kg (3,153lb). Not surprisingly, the factory also backed some cars entered in the series through its Customer Racing programme, and previewed the car in the April 2009 VLN-ADAC Westfalenfahrt at the Nürburgring, where the entries were by Schubert Motorsport. The M3 won its class (which was known as SP10 in that event) and finished thirtieth overall. On 23–24 May, an entry in the Nürburgring 24 Hours event saw the GT4 come third in class behind a pair of Aston Martins, and forty-seventh overall; the drivers were Jörg Müller, Andy Priaulx and motor sports journalist Jochen Übler.

Central to the car was a race-developed version of the S65 V8 engine that developed 485bhp (491PS) and was known as the P65 type. This was managed by an ECU 408 electronic control unit, developed in-house by BMW Motorsport. The Motorsport engineers had also come up with their own central control unit called the POWER400 that operated all the car's accessories, such as lights and wipers, through two bus systems. This not only reduced weight by eliminating traditional fuses and relays but also improved reliability.

Substantial weight reduction was only to be expected, and the coupé-style body made use of multiple lightweight CFRP panels. During the design and development stages, CFD (computational fluid dynamics) and wind-tunnel analysis, among other Formula 1 techniques, made sure that the car was as aerodynamically efficient as possible. Considerably widened tracks were also to be expected in a track racer, and to meet the ALMS regulations, the front air intakes were fitted with restrictors (each 29.4mm/1.56in in diameter)

The E92 Coupés made their first competition appearance in the American Le Mans Series for 2009.
BRIAN SNELSON/WIKIMEDIA

**US artist Jeff Koons painted a racing M3 GT2 for the Le Mans event in 2010,
to create the seventeenth in the BMW Art Car series.**

that ensured the engine's maximum power remained below 500bhp.

The ALMS cars were campaigned on BMW's behalf by Team RLL (Rahal Letterman Lanigan Racing, co-owned by former racing driver Bobby Rahal, late-night TV host David Letterman and Mi-Jack crane systems co-owner Mike Lanigan). They raced in the GT2 class – and are therefore often described as M3 GT2 types – and claimed their first victory at Road America. They then went on to finish the season in third place, behind Ferrari F430GTs and the winning Porsche 997 GTS3 cars. In 2010, Team RLL won the GT team and manufacturer championships, with podium finishes in eight of the nine races, and in the 2011 ALMS series they won the GT class again and gained the team title and driver titles for Joey Hand and Dirk Müller. The 2012 season finished with BMW Team RLL in second place behind Corvette Racing, runners-up in 2011. However, BMW Z4 cars replaced the M3s for the 2013 in the RLL Team for that season's ALMS.

THE EARLY EUROPEAN ENTRIES

Meanwhile, M3s were beginning to make waves in European motor sport events. Schnitzer Motorsport entered two cars at the Spa 1,000km in 2009 and came away with a fourth place. Then at the 2010 Nürburgring 24hrs, the M3 GT2 took an overall win in the hands of Jörg Müller, Augusto Farfus, Pedro Lamy and Uwe Alzen. Also in 2010, US artist Jeff Koons turned his attention to an M3 that entered that year's Le Mans 24hrs event. This car raced as number 79, and became the seventeenth in BMW's famous Art Cars series. At the Spa 24hrs event, the M3 driven by Andy Priaulx, Dirk Müller and Dirk Werner showed up well until suspension failure about half an hour before the end of the race put the car out of contention and allowed Porsches to take the podium places.

M3s also appeared in the ILMC (Intercontinental Le Mans

Cup) series that was new for 2010, and in November that year it was an M3 that won the GT2 class in the 1,000km race at Zhuhai, no doubt making an important contribution to sales of the car in that newly developing market.

THE M3 DTM, 2012

Success on the tracks in the USA was an important element in upholding the M3's image among US customers, but getting the M3 back into the competition limelight in Europe remained an important goal for BMW. Nowhere was it more important to achieve competition glory than in the company's home market of Germany, where there was a great deal of prestige at stake and competition machinery from Mercedes-AMG and Audi was threatening to undermine the M3's image.

So the M division focused its efforts on developing a car that would outclass its rivals in the German Touring Car Championship, or DTM (Deutsche Tourenwagen Meisterschaft). Not until their confidence in the car was high enough did BMW announce their new M3 contender.

It was indeed vitally important. Not since 1992 had BMW fielded a 'works' entry in the DTM. BMW thought that announcing their intentions early was important, too, and revealed the first iteration of the DTM car – officially at this stage a 'concept' – in mid-July 2011 when the car went on display at BMW Welt in Munich. A few days later, the company followed up with the names of the first two drivers who had signed to the 'works' DTM team.

Everything about the DTM concept was finished to the very highest standards, although the blue paint on the brake calipers was a little unnecessary for racing purposes.

BMW unveiled its DTM concept car – a silhouette racer based on the E92 M3 Coupé – over the summer of 2011.

The latest DTM regulations insisted that a certain number of components in the race cars should be the same as those in the production models, but that did not prevent the M3 DTM Concept from looking quite radically different from the production M3 of the time. The two-door coupé bodywork, finished in black all over to add to its menacing appearance, was a monocoque constructed from CFRP with an all-steel roll cage around the driving compartment. It was longer, wider and lower than the production car, and boasted a low front end with special aerodynamic racing spoiler, plus a massive wing spoiler at the rear. These helped to make it a whole 160mm (6.3in) longer than a standard M3, while huge

Testing... the DTM concept had some way to go before it was race-ready, and here it is during a shakedown run.

widened wheel arches increased its width by 146mm (5.7in) to 1,950mm (76.8in) and ground-hugging aerodynamics plus a low roof reduced overall height to a mere 1,200mm (47.2in), or 224mm (8.8in) lower than a showroom-standard M3 Coupé.

Under the front-end bodywork was not the 4.4-litre version of the V8 that had already appeared in the M3 GTS and M3 CRT cars, but rather a 480PS derivative of the 4.0-litre V8 from the regular-production models, known to BMW engineers as the P66 type and boasting maximum torque of 500Nm (369lb ft). In line with DTM regulations, this engine was restricted to two 28mm (1.1in) diameter air intakes, but, claimed BMW, the M3 DTM was still capable of accelerating from 0 to 100km/h (62mph) in around 3 seconds and of a top speed of around 300km/h (186mph).

The power was put down through a four-plate Sachs car-bon-fibre clutch and a six-speed sequential racing gearbox. There were H&R coil springs all round, and the rear suspension had been completely redesigned as a double-wishbone system with pushrods and adjustable dampers, which had six different settings, adjustable to suit the characteristics of the track where the car was being raced. The forged aluminium wheels had an 18-inch diameter, but that was their only similarity to those on the production cars: the front pair had 12-inch rims and the rear pair 13-inch rims, and of course the tyres were special racing types.

However, BMW warned at the media launch of the new car that it was likely to change quite significantly before the start of the 2012 DTM series. Track testing had only begun at the beginning of July, and modifications would depend on how the car performed. As the new director of BMW Motorsport, Jens Marquardt, explained:

Getting a new racing programme up and running is a bit like doing a jigsaw. New pieces are added almost every day, and we must put them together to create the big picture. The BMW M3 DTM Concept Car is an important milestone on our route to the start of the 2012 season. The rollout of the car was successful, and we are now starting our test programme out on the track.

In mid-July, BMW also announced that three teams would be racing M3s in the 2012 DTM. These would be BMW Team Schnitzer, BMW Team RBM and BMW Team RMG. On 17 July, the first two drivers were revealed as former World Touring Car Champion Andy Priaulx from Britain and Brazilian BMW GT veteran Augusto Farfus. Both were longstanding BMW drivers (Priaulx had most recently driven in

the ALMS for Team RLL), and both were later allocated to Team RBM. The other drivers were announced later as Martin Tomczyk and Joey Hand (another ALMS veteran) with Team RMG, and Bruno Spengler and Dirk Werner with Team Schnitzer. It promised to be an exciting season.

In fact, it could hardly have been better. Bruno Spengler (a Canadian national, despite his German-sounding name) won the second race of the 2012 DTM season for Team Schnitzer at the Lausitzring track, and went on to enjoy a spectacular season with the M3 DTM, finishing with the drivers' title. BMW Team Schnitzer won the team title and BMW also took overall honours in the manufacturers' championship. After 20 years away from the DTM, it was exactly the result that the M3s needed to reinforce their legendary status. Most important to BMW was that this result greatly enhanced their status on their home soil: with 346 points,

Pit work: Augusto Farfus' Team RBM car is seen during a pit stop during the 2013 DTM season. Note the built-in jacks that lift the car swiftly to permit tyre-changing in minimum time.

Another scene from the 2013 DTM series: Farfus was known to the BMW team affectionately as 'Gustl', and his Brazilian nationality was always to the fore.

they had finished 11 points ahead of Audi and 17 points ahead of Mercedes-Benz in the manufacturers' championship. It was the fourth time BMW had won the DTM manufacturers' title, and the third time with an M3.

For the 2013 DTM season, BMW expanded its entry from three teams and six cars to four teams and eight cars. Spengler and Werner were again the drivers for Team Schnitzer; Farfus moved to Team RMG to join Joey Hand; the Team RMG drivers were Tomczyk and Priaulx; and the fourth pair of cars was run by Team MTK with Marco Wittmann and Timo Glock as drivers. But this time, the DTM M3s found it much harder to fight off intense competition from the teams fielded by Audi and Mercedes-Benz AMG.

Spengler started the season strongly but was soon put out of contention for the drivers' championship when collisions prevented him from finishing in three rounds. Farfus never-

theless kept BMW in contention and was at the wheel of the winning car at Zandvoort – the fiftieth win for BMW in the DTM series since 1987. One more win by Timo Glock in the final round at Hockenheim in October made it fifty-one for BMW, but by this stage it was too late to secure the drivers' title. Farfus finished as runner-up for 2013.

Yet it had been a good season for the M3s. With five wins, four pole positions and four fastest laps, the BMWs carried off the Manufacturers' Championship for the second year running. They were 22 points ahead of Audi and a massive 103 points ahead of Mercedes-Benz. An added bonus was that BMW Team Schnitzer took the Best Pit Stop Award 2013, given by tyre manufacturer Hankook. So the M3 DTM cars went out on a high note, but 2013 would be their last season in the series. For 2014, BMW would campaign the new M4 DTM Coupé in their place.

Oschersleben, 15 September 2013: the M3 DTM cars battle it out on the track with their rivals from Audi and Mercedes. Farfus was in the green Team RBM car, and went on to win this round of the championship.

ABOVE: **More scenes from Oschersleben, 2013: the white Team Schnitzer car was driven by Dirk Werner...**

RIGHT: **... and the yellow Team MTK car by Timo Glock.**

TOP: **Farfus, car and jubilant support team after the 2013 Oschersleben event.**

BELOW: **Final race of the 2013 season: Timo Glock's M3 leads at Hockenheim.**

The cars on the Hockenheim track during practice for the last event of the 2013 season. The green car was driven by Farfus, the red and white one by Priaulx, and the blue and white one by Werner.

TOP: **Bruno Spengler (right) congratulates Timo Glock on his win at the final event of the 2013 DTM season.**

BELOW: **The BMW DTM teams line up for a victory photograph at the end of the 2013 DTM season. An E30 M3 from the BMW Museum collection completes the picture.**

THE E90-SERIES M3 IN ITS OWN TIME

It is easy to underestimate the impact that a high-performance car like the M3 had on buyers when it was new. Rival manufacturers are constantly raising their game to compete, and some of the more recent Mercedes-AMG and Audi models have edged the E90-series M3 out of the limelight to some extent. So how exactly did the cars appear when they were new? This selection of quotations from the motoring media of the time is a reminder that the M3 was indeed highly regarded – even if some writers had their doubts.

Car, online, 12 July 2007
(The car tested was a Coupé with six-speed manual gearbox.)

The new car needs to be a brilliant all-round package, capable of pleasing those who like the idea of the badge more than what it first stood for: track-honed thrills. And it is very, very good. This car is fast, practical, well built, comfortable and safe. But in trying to hit so many targets, the E92 leaves purists wanting. Just like back in 1992, the E92 will leave the hardcore craving more ... And the V8 does significantly alter the M3's character. Where before a creamy straight-six throatiness was followed by the trademark metallic rasp towards peak rpms, now a nice woofly warble under lighter throttle loads precedes a hard-edged – if more muted – charge for the redline. The spine-tingling zinginess of the E46 car is gone, replaced by a more mature, if still exhilarating, progression. Unsurprisingly, the quest for a high-revving engine has left a hole in the torque low down, so you need to stir that six-speed manual ... to really get moving. The 'box is carried over from the E46 and obviously shares its characteristics: direct but a little arthritic.

Turn-in still feels a bit dumbed down and numb. Understeer was never an issue in the last car – it just dived into a corner with razor-sharp precision. The new M3 has a little more roll on turn-in, and you can feel the loads building on the front tyre as forces increase... As you'd expect, less focused handling does improve the ride quality significantly with the M3 soaking up bumps much better than its predecessor ever did.

All that extra power – nearly 80bhp up from last time – does mean the traction control intervenes more frequently, but it's rarely intrusive and keen drivers can reduce its role with a press of the M button.

As before, rear legroom is nothing more than adequate so six footers sitting behind six footers will feel cramped.

Evo, August 2007
(The car tested was a standard M3 Coupé fitted with the optional EDC system.)

With the possible exception of the engine, which is more spectacular than we'd dared hope, the new M3 has thrown us no great surprises. It's quicker – much quicker – than the car it replaces, and more hardcore in its delivery.

The only disappointment is that the engine sounds better from the outside than the inside, bystanders treated to an incredible, punchy, hard-as-nails howl while you're left with no option but to wind the windows down to enjoy the full effect.

The clutch is light and progressive but the gearshift has that typical slightly springy BMW feel, and if you're less than smooth when working on and off the throttle you'll also induce some clumsy-feeling on-off shunt in traffic ... [but] Every gear presents you with the opportunity to enjoy a seamless, savage surge from tickover to the red line ... there's little body roll and ... all indications are that body control is far better without any penalty in ride comfort.

The chassis' balance is pleasingly neutral, with plenty of front-end grip to lean on as you begin to feed-in the abundant power of the high-revving V8 ... [but] ... it's easy to awaken the stability control even in its most relaxed mode. Fortunately when you disengage the system the M3 remains intuitive and easily steered on the throttle ... More steering feel wouldn't go amiss, but the M3 works happily at or beyond the limit.

One big improvement is the eradication of the infamous M3 fidget, which would often have you bouncing gently in your seat as the car seemed to get out of phase with the road surface.

The cockpit is of good quality, but it lacks the special ambience of a focused drivers' car. The excessively fat-rimmed steering wheel provides a tac-tile clue to the M3's sporting role, and the seats are supportive as well as comfortable, but in every other respect the interior is a rather uninspiring place to be.

Autocar, 2007

It's the car's ability to transform from being practical (but potent) into a thrill-a-minute ride that marks it out as special.

[The V8] is an exceptional motor with a breadth of performance that is truly impressive ... When using the six-speed manual, the shift feels unhelpful at first and the clutch too abrupt, but ... familiarity breeds smoothness ... The slightly more frugal seven-speed automatic ... rather undermines the point of buying such a car in the first place, even if it does make the M3 a quicker car in a straight line as well.

The cabin oozes class, but it emphasises the car's everyday practicality far more than it does the mighty performance that is just a stab of the right foot away ... The driving position isn't without fault and includes one major irritation: you sit too high. M engineers insist that the squab material compresses about an inch over the first three weeks of ownership, but even that's not enough ... Otherwise it's an extremely comfortable place to sit. Rear occupants have enough legroom for one six-footer to sit behind another, and the boot is vast.

The convertible's roof arrangement adds more weight, at the slight – but evident – cost of handling precision ... [but] ... don't think that by opting for the four-door saloon you are going to be forced to give much away. The extra practicality that this car offers leads you to expect some kind of compromise in its handling; if it's bigger inside, you guess it must be bigger outside, heavier, somehow less sharp. But it just isn't.

The others, in particular Audi, have all but caught the once uncatchable M3, but for those who love rear-driven machinery, this is still the best practical performance car on sale.

Evo, April 2010
(The car on test had the new Competition Package.)

For the umpteenth time though BMW, the steering wheel rim does not have to be as fat as a Bratwurst. It really doesn't help.

The sharper front end seems to add even more turn-in grip, allowing you to bring the rear end into play on corner entry. However, the M3 Competition simply isn't as playful and adjustable as the M3 Edition we drove last summer. In short it's got too much grip, and the blame for that can be laid at the door of the Michelin Pilot Sport tyres. The Conti CSC3's that are the other OE fitment (you don't get to choose which your car comes on on) have lower limits, but a more manageable grip/slip balance that suits the M3 to a tee ... Nevertheless, we're talking small differences, and the M3 Competition does have that bit more edge, helping make it more addictive than ever.

Autocar, 6 July 2010
(The car tested was an M3 GTS.)

Fire the M3 GTS's new V8 and you're immediately made aware of all the under bonnet tinkering as it catches and settles into a lumpy idle overlaid with a pulsating exhaust note that is full of purpose and fantastically naughty. ... At lower revs, the M3 GTS feels more muscular than the standard M3 – not a lot but enough to make you think the engine changes have been worth the effort.

What sets the GTS apart most from the standard M3 is its sharpness. Everything you ask of the new coupé is carried out with greater immediacy, added response and heightened accuracy. The steering is heavenly – heavier than the standard power assisted hydraulic set-up, but the added effort that's required is more than made up for in precision. Turn-in is instant. There's no slack as you come off centre, just eager, linear response.

Even at high speeds the M3 GTS remains wonderfully flat and neutral during cornering, and with

SO YOU WANT TO BUY AN E90-SERIES M3?

As these words were being written in late 2013, the oldest E90-series M3 was seven years old and the last ones had still not passed through the showrooms to their first owners. So it would be reasonable to assume that more problems will come to light as the cars get older and rack up bigger mileages.

At the outset, it is important to remember that this generation of M3 models could be had with a large variety of optional equipment, and that how much of that equipment there is on any individual car may make a big difference to its asking price. Also worth remembering is that the M3 was not intended to be serviced at regular intervals, but instead used inputs from various major components to its own on-board computer to determine when a service was due. Hard use demanded more frequent services than more gentle driving. As a result, the service documents may reveal a rather odd pattern of maintenance, which, in itself, does not have to be a cause for concern. However, it is important to check, as far as possible, that no servicing has been missed.

One important item to check in a car's documents is whether the initial 1,000-mile service was carried out when it should have been. This is very important to the long-term health of the engine, because the cars came from BMW with special running-in fluids that had to be changed at that mileage. Major delays in changing them may have led to excessive wear, which will eventually become apparent as a durability issue.

The V8 engine is generally long-lived if treated properly, but it's worth knowing that the oil cannot be checked in the traditional way with a dipstick: the engine does not have one. Instead, the oil level is checked through the iDrive system, and it is not unknown for this to give false readings. Regular oil changes are essential, and many owners have the oil changed after relatively low mileages as an insurance against problems.

Owners frequently comment on two issues associated with the V8 engine. The first is that it is thirsty – and can be much thirstier than the older straight-six M3 engines if used hard. Typically, a full tank of petrol will last for around 300 miles, but fuel consumption in the low 'teens is a distinct possibility if the car is driven hard. The second comment is that the engine is quiet, and makes very different noises from the older 6-cylinder types. This has encouraged some owners to fit aftermarket exhausts that give a more satisfying V8 'rumble' but which some people find take noise levels too high. Worth investigating is the M Performance exhaust system that BMW introduced as an aftermarket option in autumn 2010, not least because it will not invalidate the car's warranty.

A lot has been said (especially on enthusiasts' forums) about the DCT transmission. It is not as smooth as a conventional automatic, but it does give extremely fast gear changes that no average human driver can emulate. Some owners have complained of a 'lag' in selecting gears, and others have not noticed any such thing. It seems probable that a software update introduced around autumn 2008 to overcome a reluctance to change down on early transmissions may have introduced a one- or two-second delay, noticeable especially when kicking down to second gear. Subsequent software updates rectified the problem, so it is advisable to check that a DCT-equipped car has the latest updates. It is also advisable to be wary of any transmission that does not change down on demand.

The six-speed manual gearboxes generally give no cause for concern, although fluid leaks may suggest hard use. Some cars suffer from noisy differentials at parking speeds, a problem caused by the limited-slip differential, which can usually be cured by changing the oil. It is best to take specialist advice on the right oil to use.

Handling and roadholding should be extraordinarily good, and any cause for concern needs careful investigation: the suspension geometry can go out of alignment. Hard kerbing can be one cause, and this will also cause damage to wheels. One suspiciously new-looking wheel may be a clue that a replacement has been necessary! Opinions differ, but many people claim that the car rides better on the standard 18-inch wheels than on the optional 19-inch size. Tyres will be expensive, so check for wear and watch out for cheap replacements.

The brakes are extremely good in everyday use, but in fast driving over long distances or on the track they begin to lose their bite. Some owners who drive their cars hard have upgraded to harder pads or made more comprehensive changes using aftermarket brake components. One way or another, most M3s get through standard pads and even discs relatively quickly.

The bodywork will probably not suffer from anything

SO YOU WANT TO BUY AN E90-SERIES M3? *continued*

worse than stone chips in the paint, but it is worth checking all round for minor damage or repairs. Front-end collision damage needs to be repaired by a specialist because the bonnet panel is made of aluminium and the front wings of plastic; neither takes kindly to back-street repair jobs, and the evidence of such repairs is usually only too visible. On Convertibles, never forget to check that the power-operated roof operates correctly and smoothly in both directions.

One particular weakness seems to lie in the interior, where some experts argue that the materials used were cheaper and less durable than on earlier M3s. The main issue is premature wear, especially of the upholstery and in particular of the front seat side bolsters. The leather can wrinkle in places, which makes it rough to the touch, but most other wear problems can be put right with conditioner or by a leather specialist.

---

the DSC ... switched into M-mode there's rarely any intervention. ... The new BMW will eventually understeer. But with a good deal of commitment and DSC switched off you can drive around it. The limits are so high, though, you'd likely never get near them on public roads.

Evo, July 2010
(The car tested was an M3 GTS.)

The combination of DCT transmission, front-engine/ rear-drive and excellent stability systems make it easier to drive than a Porsche 911 GT3 RS. The brakes are the first on an M Car to match the straight line performance, a good thing.

The GTS is a great drive, but in pure, objective terms, it just doesn't justify the price. It should have been £75k and they should have made 1,000 of them. Then Porsche would have had one hell of a fright.

[The GTS] struggles for traction next to the Porsche, doesn't steer as sweetly and isn't as fast – in a straight line or in terms of lap time. I found myself enjoying it immensely because it takes that age-old M3 trick – being able to carve a neat line one lap and then providing hilarious, smokey slides the next – and moves it a stage further. The nagging doubt remains though, that a BMW M3 Competition with a half cage, some sticky rubber, new suspension, bigger brakes, some noisy pipes and a re-map mightn't be all that different. And the work wouldn't cost £50k to complete.

Evo, November 2012
(The car tested was an M3 CRT.)

The almost Q-car subtle looks certainly don't advertise that you've spent Bentley money on your M3.

[Driving the car is] Brilliant. You instantly feel the stiffer suspension and tighter body control, but there is still that extra confidence that you get with the saloon. The front end isn't quite so unwilling to relinquish its grip as the coupé and as a result it feels like it has slightly more neutral balance and it's easier to judge grip levels. The engine is magnificent and the reduced sound deadening lets the wonderfully rasping exhaust note permeate the cabin perfectly.

Automobile (online), June 2013
(The car tested was a Lime Rock Park Edition.)

An orange M3 gets noticed, let me tell you. On my way home from a quick trip to IKEA, a couple of young guys in a last-generation Mazda 6 came up alongside me on I-94 and were clearly waiting for me to demonstrate the car's capabilities.

I couldn't very well ignore a challenge from a Mazda 6, now could I? I waited a few beats and then the freeway opened up with three empty lanes. I hit the M and Power buttons for a very discernible power boost, downshifted to third, and floored it. The speedometer indicated 130mph before I or the Mazda 6 guys even knew what happened. For about 30 seconds, I owned westbound I-94. I slowed down, entered the middle lane, and waited for the Mazda guys to catch up. They seemed happy. I know I was.

THE FIFTH GENERATION

Just as this book was being completed in December 2013, BMW announced the fifth generation of its high-performance compact model with deliveries due to start in 2014. As expected, the car came as an M3 Saloon or an M4 Coupé; the new 3 Series had been developed as the four-door car with the code of F30, and the related two-door cars had been developed as the 4 Series under the code of F32.

One key reason for developing the two cars under separate nameplates was the arrival of the Audi A5 Coupé as a separate model from the A4 Saloon on which it was based: BMW had to compete. The two models were manufactured in different plants, too: while the M3 Saloon was built at the Regensburg plant where all M3s had been built since 1992,

assembly of the M4 Coupé was carried out in Munich, home of the original E30 M3.

Central to the thinking behind the new M3 and M4 was weight reduction, and both cars came with aluminium wings and bonnet and a carbon-reinforced plastic (CFRP) roof. While the M3 Saloon made do with a special lip spoiler at the rear, the M4 Coupé had a lightweight CFRP boot lid with an integral spoiler. Many suspension components on both cars were aluminium, and even the standard engine strut brace was made of CFRP.

Airflow management had been another central pillar of the M3/M4 concept. So alongside existing features like the aerodynamic twin-stalk door mirrors, the air channelled

Instantly recognizable as a BMW, and with design cues that make is instantly recognizable as a product of the M Division, this is the fifth-generation M3, an F30 salon.

As always, exquisite detail touches added to the appeal fo the M models.

through the oil cooler created a venturi effect that in turn reduced front-axle lift. The M side gills had integrated Air Breathers and helped to minimize turbulence in the front wheel arches.

For the engine, BMW went back to the in-line 6-cylinder for which they had become famous – but with a twist. The new 3.0-litre came with M Twin Power Turbo technology, which in practice meant a pair of single-scroll turbochargers plus an indirect intercooler. Direct petrol injection, VALVE-TRONIC variable valve timing and a Double-VANOS system were part of the package, along with an oil control system that meant each and every engine was track-ready. Weight was pared off by sprayed-on cylinder liners and reciprocating weight was reduced by a lightweight forged crankshaft.

However, character had been engineered in too: electronically controlled flaps in the exhaust system reduced back pressure and could be adjusted to give precisely the sort of sound that M3 enthusiasts had come to love. BMW claimed that the new engine delivered 431PS between 5,500 and 7,300rpm and was red-lined at 7,600rpm – very high for a turbocharged engine. Torque meanwhile was more than 40 per cent greater than in the 4.0-litre V8 of the previous generation cars, with 550Nm (406lb ft) available all the way from 1,850 to 5,500rpm. Better yet, CO_2 emissions from the new engine were more than 25 per cent lower than those of the V8 it replaced.

The standard gearbox was a six-speed manual with lightweight, twin-plate clutch, and electronics arranged to blip the throttle on downshifts to give smoother changes, as had already been seen in the DCT transmission. The alternative gearbox was, of course, a seven-speed DCT, featuring Launch Control and Drivelogic. Among its new features was Stability Clutch Control, which opened the clutch to help reduce understeer when the car's electronic systems detected it. All models came with an Active M Differential, and there were selectable drive modes that were activated through an M Drive Manager system with button control on the steering wheel.

Inevitably, the precise specification differed from one country to the next. For the UK, however, BMW had focused on raising equipment levels. So Adaptive M suspension was now standard, along with M Compound brakes, and the standard wheels were 19-inch forged alloys with a Ferric Grey or Jet Black finish.

As for the figures that matter to M3 (and now M4) enthusiasts, both cars could despatch the 0–100km/h (0–62mph) sprint in 4.3 seconds with a manual gearbox or 4.1 seconds with the DCT transmission. The 155mph (250km/h) governed maximum was still in place, but no doubt the speed limiter could be removed to order... and all that came with fuel consumption of 32.1mpg with the manual gearbox and 34mpg with the DCT. These successors to the great M3s of earlier years were certainly destined to lead the pack once again.

Supportive front seats in an M3 saloon.

The M3 and M4 dashboards were, inevitably, based on the standard F30 and F32 types.

For the engine, the fifth-generation cars went back to a straight-six, this time with twin turbochargers.

The huge font air intakes help to identify this version of the F32 coupé as an M4.

INDEX